Israel...It's Complicated
Teacher Resource Guide

Lessons by Irit Eliav Levin

Foreword by Richard Walter,
Center for Israel Education

Additional Resources edited
by Behrman House staff

Behrman House
www. behrmanhouse.com

Behrman House, Inc.
Millburn, New Jersey 07041
www.behrmanhouse.com

ISBN 978-0-87441-983-2

Printed in the United States of America

Design: Tim Holtz
Project manager: Aviva Gutnick
Editorial consultant: Judith Sandman

Lesson on page 94 by Richard Walter, Center for Israel Education

Contents

Foreword

by Richard Walter, Center for Israel Education

Teaching our students about Israel empowers them with the story of Jewish self-determination, which shapes the future of the Jewish people. At the Center for Israel Education, we believe that Israel and Zionism are about Jews becoming the subject of their own story rather than being the object of someone else's.

As a teen participant in a recent CIE program said, "Israel is the embodiment of freedom and the embodiment of Judaism." Effective Israel education should begin with this core concept, and as Hillel said, "the rest is commentary."

Educating students about modern Israel is not an easy task. It presents numerous challenges, including our personal and political biases, where to devote our energies, and how to help our students truly understand the country's many complexities.

Challenging does not mean impossible, however. Here are three strategies you can focus on for effective Israel education:

First, focus on the broad concepts like ensuring the future, of returning to our ancestral homeland, and of self-governance, the centrality of the land of Israel to the Jewish people, and the concept that Israel is a complex laboratory for living a Jewish life in the modern world. Use facts and stories to emphasize these concepts, not the other way around. Don't try to cover every historical fact. You are teaching students grades 6–7, not a university seminar.

Second, don't assume you need to teach Israel only as its own unit or grade level curriculum. Too often in our work with educators we hear, "Fifth grade is our Israel year." Israel relates to all aspects of Jewish life. Think about all the ways you can integrate Israel into the many topics you teach and across many grades. For example, when I teach about Tu Bishevat, I have my students begin with the debate between Hillel and Shammai as to whether the holiday should be marked on the first or the fifteenth of the month of Shevat. I then show them monthly rainfall charts in Jerusalem and Tel Aviv and ask them to determine who was right in choosing the date that, according to the Talmud, should be when "most of the year's rains have already fallen." Connecting the festival to these debates about Jewish life that were taking place in Israel makes the country relevant in new ways.

Finally, focus on the positive. While a lot of Israel's complexity is about the country's challenges, there is much to celebrate. Remember that Israel, like any country, is not a finished product. As a maturing nation, it is still learning to deal with many of the complexities laid out in this guide. But when we only present Israel in the context of anti-Semitism and what others have done to the Jewish people, we fail to help our students understand the importance of self-determination and choice.

Before using these materials, I suggest that you craft a vision for Israel education for yourself and your students. This need not, and should not, be a personal process. Engaging clergy, colleagues, parents, alumni, and others from your school and community in the process will help you identify and map out a plan for Israel education in your school.

In framing your vision, ensure that students gain an essential understanding of Israel's place in the historic, cultural, political, and religious development of the Jewish people so that you can address contemporary complexities, such as the Arab-Israeli conflict, in a developmentally appropriate way.

Other considerations when using this resource guide:

- Allow students to develop and form their own opinions about Israel.
- Identify those aspects of Israel that particularly resonate with your students and use them to help build students' knowledge about other areas. For example, we can learn a great deal about Israeli culture or immigration history through the country's music or literature.
- Use original sources wherever possible, even if they are difficult for students to totally comprehend. A variety of original sources are included in this guide and in the *Israel... It's Complicated* student book, and others are suggested for use in this guide. Do not be afraid to use them to challenge your students. They are working with these types of materials in their secular schools, and we should also be using them in our classrooms.
- Educate yourself and don't be afraid of what you do not know. There are numerous websites and organizations, including the Center for Israel Education, devoted to helping Jewish educators improve their personal knowledge of Israel and develop new strategies for teaching it to students of all ages. Take part in workshops, webinars, and other forums to fill in your personal knowledge gaps. At the same time, don't be afraid to respond to a student's question with, "I don't know. Let's find out." This allows for communal self-discovery and helps to re-emphasize that when it comes to Israel, no one has all the answers.

For more than two thousand years, Jews have collectively prayed for a return to Zion. We should guide students to form their own opinions by providing content and context, using primary sources when possible. Our aim as Israel educators should be to create critical thinkers, not followers, no matter our personal politics. We should not be afraid if our students ultimately form a different relationship with Israel than their teachers, parents, or grandparents. As North American Jews we can move forward by educating ourselves and our communities to create understanding and dialogue. Our past, present, and future as Jews is inextricably linked with Israel.

The mission of the Center for Israel Education is to educate broadly about modern Israel, relying on primary sources. The Center, housed on the campus of Emory University, has four primary goals: 1. Promote the ongoing concept that Israel is an integral and essential part of modern Jewish history; 2. Provide students, educators, and life-long learners with materials and trustworthy sources to engage with others about modern Israel; 3. Train students and adults to become literate in the study of modern Israel by understanding the concepts of state-seeking, state-making, and state-keeping; 4. Build digital resources, conduct workshops, webinars and on-line learning opportunities.

Overview

Israel...It's Complicated and this accompanying Teacher Resource Guide are designed to give students a new approach to understanding Israel—its history, diversity, accomplishments, and challenges.

Our hope is that *Israel...It's Complicated* will be an impetus for a lifelong connection to the land and people of Israel, as students continue to appreciate and wrestle with the issues that make Israel what it is today and will continue to shape Israel in the future.

The activities are designed to help students form their own opinions, learn how to ask and answer difficult questions, and investigate unique perspectives about complicated issues. Students will use different modalities, including art, drama, videos/media, debates, and more throughout this process. Students will have the opportunity to work independently, in pairs, in small groups, and as a class to delve deeper into these issues.

Features of *Israel...It's Complicated*

Each chapter of *Israel...It's Complicated* focuses on one big idea; for example, Israel as a creative and technological force, or Israel as a place of conflict in search of peace. Recurring features include:

- **Debate It!** Each chapter encourages students to debate an issue of concern to Israelis today. Students will represent and discuss a variety of viewpoints, perspectives, and opinions. Let students know that they don't necessarily need to agree with a specific side in order to debate it.
- **What Do You See?** Draws students' attention to the eye-catching photographs in their books for a look at Israel today or the history that has shaped the land of Israel and the Jewish people.
- **Talk about It!** Asks students working independently or with partners to formulate and express personal views on issues affecting Israel and their own lives.
- **By the Numbers.** Statistics about Israel that may surprise students and spark discussion.
- **It's Complicated.** The capstone of every chapter (except 9, about tourism and voluntourism). Stimulates students to dive deeper into one of the complicated issues facing Israel and Israelis. Students will understand that for many of these issues, there are no clear-cut answers, that there is merit and value to a range of arguments.

Using This Teacher Resource Guide

This guide is designed to be flexible. You may choose to use the lessons exactly as they are, or you may decide to adapt them to fit the needs and interests of your students. You also may choose to use the Building Activities included in each lesson (see next page) or the additional resources provided with each chapter (also see next page) to craft your own lesson or supplemental activity. Activities are designed to spark meaningful conversations; these are invaluable in helping students develop their own thoughts about and relationship with Israel.

Each chapter in this guide includes the following:

Enduring Understanding: The overriding message or idea that students should understand after having studied this chapter.

Chapter Overview: A brief summary of the information that will be covered in this chapter.

Words to Know: Definitions of key terms found in the student book.

Lessons: Each chapter in the book includes one to three lessons, for a total of 23 lessons. Each lesson is designed to be about 45 minutes long. Additional time should be allotted if you plan to include Building Activities or any of the additional resources—in-class extension and enrichment activities.

Each lesson contains:

- **Essential Question**—The central question of the lesson, designed to encourage students to probe for deeper meaning in the material at hand.
- **Learning Objectives**—Goals to help you direct the learning and measure your students' progress.
- **Materials**—A list of supplies needed to complete the activities. It is assumed that basic supplies, like pens, pencils, paper, and dry-erase boards will always be available to students. These basic supplies are not listed individually in each lesson.

Additionally, some activities in *Israel...It's Complicated* and this guide include videos or other digital components that are integrated into the lesson. Access to computers, tablets, and/or smartphones will be helpful. Digital resources are available at bhlink.me/Israel, followed by the chapter number (for example, bhlink.me/israel5 will take you to the resources for chapter 5).

The lessons also occasionally ask teachers and students to print out certain materials in advance, since printers may not be accessible during class time.

- **Activities**—Each lesson opens with a short, fun activity to immediately engage students. Step-by-step information on implementing activities is followed by and potential answers to questions or debate topics.
- **Building Activities**—Optional activities to extend and expand student understanding of the lesson concepts. Building Activities may supplement or replace the material in the student text, depending on your classroom needs. These activities are untimed.
- **Reflection**—Found at the end of each chapter, designed for students to review the material covered, assess material learned, and begin to consider their own thoughts and perspectives on issues raised.
- **Teacher Tips**—Suggestions to help you best implement activities, such as how to involve families in activities or how to approach sensitive situations.

Additional Resources: Each chapter in this guide includes supplemental material, such as activities drawn from other sources, primary source documents or news articles, or helpful charts. Use these resources to enhance lessons or to craft your own lesson or activity, as time and creativity permit.

Here are six ideas for using primary source documents:

1 Have a debate.

2 Have students read the document independently, in small groups, or pairs (*chevruta*). Then have them develop three questions for the author of the article.

3 Role play.

4 Have students act as news anchors or investigators reporting on stories.

5 Have students interview each other.

6 Think-Pair-Share: Ask students to read a text to themselves and think about it. Then, have students, in groups of two or three, work together to explore and understand a text. After they have done so, invite them as a team to present their findings to the class.

Preparing Students to Use *Israel: It's Complicated*

Discussions about Israel lend themselves to strong emotions, differing political ideologies, and conflicting opinions. Make sure that your learning environment provides a safe space for open discussion to occur.

Establishing Ground Rules

Talk with students about the ground rules needed to make this learning as meaningful and rewarding as possible. Including students in setting the rules will help them feel invested in the process. For example:

- **Be respectful.** Insist that students (and the teacher) listen to one another with respect. Students should listen quietly and attentively when someone else is speaking and avoid interrupting. This demonstrates kindness and maturity.
- **Honor different perspectives.** Remind students that everyone will have different perspectives about Israel and what it means to them, and that we will respect all viewpoints.
- **Actively participate.** Students will receive the most benefit if they are willing to engage in this often complex subject matter. The more they are willing to talk, question, and consider new options, the more they will get out of this program.

Promoting and Mediating Debate

- Before introducing complicated issues, you might discuss with students that Jewish tradition values debate and even disagreement for the sake of learning.
- There are multiple strategies to engage students in a topic. You might want to build on comments students make by paraphrasing their statements. You can also elaborate on students' contributions with examples, or suggest a new idea that builds on students' thoughts and takes them to the next level.

- You might play "devil's advocate" and deliberately disagree with what a student suggests to provoke further debate. Students might become passionate about these topics, and you will find it necessary to mediate, to keep the discussion going, while diffusing any tensions that might be brewing.

Creating a Positive Learning Environment

As with any teaching opportunity, children learn better when you create a positive educational environment. Some tips to guide that process:

- Students learn in a variety of ways. Your class may include visual, aural, kinesthetic, and other types of learners. You will have students who love art and drama, students who enjoy thoughtful discussions, and students who thrive on using multimedia materials. This guide contains activities designed to approach the subject matter in a variety of ways, to provide as many different approaches to learning as possible.
- When picking pairs or groups, try to match students in a way that encourages productive learning. For example, a shy student may benefit from being paired with someone who is more assertive at answering questions.
- It is easy for friends to work together, but encouraging students to work with classmates they do not know as well may stimulate more interesting discussion and debate. Ensure that no one is left out of any of the activities.
- Engage other invested adults in the process, if possible. Communicate with families what you are learning so that they can have conversations at home. This will be especially important as parents are likely to have their own opinions both about Israel and about how their children learn about Israel. Consider creating a class website where students can upload videos of class activities to share with families. Invite your rabbi, cantor, or education director to your class to answer questions, observe the learning, or provide additional resources to support you. Check to see if your organization has any guidelines about teaching Israel that you should be aware of as you engage in this process.
- Include information on current events when appropriate. Students may benefit from placing current issues into the context provided by the book. It will give them tools to both understand what is happening and to be able to see multiple perspectives on a given issue.
- Your enthusiasm for teaching about Israel and investigating its complexities will encourage students' excitement and help them forge a strong connection to the country, its history, and its people.

Introduction What IS Israel?

Words to Know:

Canaan: Israel's biblical name during the time of Abraham and Sarah

disputed/occupied territories: name used for the west bank of the Jordan River by Palestinian families who left their homes there before the 1948 war and feel this land belongs to them (called the West Bank by this book)

Judea and Samaria: name given by religious Zionists to the West Bank because that was the name of the land during biblical times when Jews ruled there

Kingdom of Judah / Kingdom of Israel: names of the two kingdoms into which Israel split after the reign of King Solomon

Palestine: name given to the land of Israel when the Romans conquered the Jewish nation; named after the Philistines, a nation that had often fought against the Jewish people.

Introduction

Enduring Understanding:

Everything related to Israel, from its name to its borders, is complicated because different groups of people have different opinions.

Chapter Overview:

This chapter encourages students to verbalize their impressions of Israel. They will locate Israel on the map, consider the many names the land of Israel has been called throughout history, and begin to explore why the West Bank is controversial. Students will have a chance to ask questions about Israel and generate potential answers.

Introduction Lesson 1

Where and What is Israel?

Essential Question: What does Israel mean to the Jewish people and to the world?

Learning Objectives: Students will be able to:

- Express their impressions of Israel
- Recognize different names Israel has had over the years
- Locate Israel on a map
- Begin asking questions about Israel

Materials:

- poster board or large sheets of paper
- sticky notes
- highlighters
- markers

Activities

Design an Israeli Star (10 minutes)

Ask students:

When I say *United States / Canada* [depending on where you live], what are the first words that come to mind? *(Answers may include: democracy; diversity; equality; president; prime minister; Congress; Parliament; wealth; income inequality; guns; army; peace; Washington, DC; Ottawa; Statue of Liberty; immigrants; natural resources.)* Now think of Israel. What words come to mind?

Tell students:

Fill in the center of the star on page 5 of your books with the words you associate with Israel. Write the words that you most strongly associate with Israel larger, and the other words smaller. *(Possible words may include: Jewish, homeland, Hebrew, Arabic, Jerusalem, Tel Aviv, Haifa, historic, dangerous, controversial, diverse, sunny, desert, fun, tourist destination, holy, sacred, Kotel, Western Wall, Masada, Dead Sea, ancient, modern.)*

Then, with a partner, answer the following questions:

- Take a look at the words you chose. How many are positive words? How many are negative?
- What made you choose those words? *(Answers may include media influence, personal experience with Israel or Israelis, previous courses, books read, etc.)*
- Exchange stars with your partner. Which words do you have in common? Which are different?
- How different would the words be if you were f illing in the star with words that describe the place you live?
- If you could add words about Israel to your star or take them away after seeing other stars, what would you change?

Building Activity: Where is Israel?

Have students read "Where Is Israel? How Big Is It?" and complete "Map It: Where's Israel?" on page 6. Then, distribute blank Middle East maps (found on page 11 of this guide) and ask students to do the following:

- Use highlighters to fill in the area that is Israel.
- Write in the names of the countries that share a border with Israel. *(Students can use maps on pages 6 and 8 of their books for reference. Those countries include Egypt, Jordan, Syria, and Lebanon.)*
- Draw waves under the bodies of water that touch Israel. *(These bodies include the Mediterranean Sea, the Red Sea, the Jordan River, Lake Kinneret [Sea of Galilee or Lake Tiberias], and the Dead Sea.)*
- What do you notice about Israel's size now that you see it in relation to its neighbors? *(Students will likely comment on Israel's small size.)*
- What else do you notice on the map? What do you wonder about? *(Students may notice that Israel is surrounded by Arab countries. They might be surprised by the size of the Red Sea or the Mediterranean Sea. They might comment on how narrow Israel is compared to other countries.)*

Map It: Create Your Own (15 minutes)

Say to students:

> Look at the *Cloverleaf Map* found on page 7. *(A full version of the map is found at bhlink.me/Israel1.)* With a partner, answer the following three questions:

1. What places do you recognize on this map? *(Answers include: England, Europe, Poland, Denmark, Syria, Asia, India, Persia, Jerusalem, Egypt, Libya, Africa, etc.)*
2. What places seem especially important from the map? *(Students will likely say Jerusalem, Europe, Asia, and Africa.)*

3 The artist placed Jerusalem at the center of his map. What cities might people today put at the center of their maps? *(A few possibilities include Bethlehem; Mecca; Washington D.C.; New York; Paris; London; Beijing; Jerusalem.)*

After students have answered the questions, say:

> In the blank cloverleaf found on page 7 of your books, imagine that you are creating a map of the world today. What countries or continents would you include? What place would be at the center? *(Students may pick any city, country, or continent, depending on what they wish to highlight as a priority.)*

Students should discuss their maps with their partners and explain why they made the choices they did in the creative process. What role did Jerusalem play in their maps? *(Some students may continue to highlight Jerusalem. Others may not include Jerusalem at all.)*

Gallery of Questions (20 minutes)

Ask students to each think of three questions they have about Israel and write them on page 9 of their books. Then, in small groups, students should share their questions, choose three that they find most interesting, write them on a poster board or large sheet of paper, and post on the walls.

Teacher Tip: Remind students that this is a safe space to ask their questions; they should be respectful of the questions posed by their classmates.

Invite students to walk around the room reading all the questions. Using sticky notes, students should add:

- New questions they have that were inspired by the questions on the posters
- Ideas for possible answers to the questions
- One-word responses about how the questions make them feel (happy, angry, worried, proud, etc.)

Once everyone has posted their notes, invite students to walk around the room and read them. Then, come back and ask these three questions:

1 What questions surprised you?

2 Were there are any questions you'd like to add to your own lists *[students can write them in the box under their first set of questions]*

3 How can you find answers to your questions as you use this book and learn about Israel? *[Refer students to the resources available at bhlink.me/israel1, encourage them to read books and watch movies about Israel, talk to others about their own experiences with Israel, etc.]*

Teacher Tip: It may be helpful to keep the posters and reference them as the class progresses, ensuring that as many questions as possible are answered.

Additional Resources

The following activities and information can supplement the lessons or be used on their own to enrich introductory learning about Israel.

Timeline of Israel's History

EARLY JEWISH HISTORY

1700 BCE	Famine forces Israelites to migrate to Egypt
1250–1200 BCE	Exodus from Egypt, entry into Canaan
1030–1010 BCE	Reign of King Saul
1010–970 BCE	Reign of King David, Jerusalem becomes capital
970–931 BCE	Reign of King Solomon, First Temple
931 BCE	Secession of Northern Kingdom (Israel) from Southern Kingdom (Judah)
722–721 BCE	Assyrians destroy Israel, ten tribes exiled
587–586 BCE	Judah and First Temple destroyed, Babylonian exile
538 BCE	Edict of Cyrus, first return from exile
520–515 BCE	Second Temple built
333–331 BCE	Alexander the Great conquers Palestine
166–160 BCE	Maccabean revolt
142–129 BCE	Jewish autonomy under Hasmoneans

THE RISE OF CHRISTIANITY

63 BCE	Rome annexes Palestine
37–4 BCE	Herod the Great, king of Judea
4 BCE–30 CE	Jesus
36–64 CE	Paul the Apostle
50–125 CE	New Testament writings

66–73 CE	Great Revolt against Rome
70 CE	Destruction of Jerusalem and the Second Temple
73 CE	Last stand of Jews at Masada
132–135 CE	Bar-Kokhba Revolt
200 CE	Mishnah (Oral Law) compiled and edited
312–313 CE	Constantine embraces Christianity
380–391 CE	Christianity becomes religion of Roman Empire

ISLAM BECOMES AN EMPIRE

570	Muhammad's birth
622	Hegira, Muhammad flees persecution in Mecca
638	Jews permitted by Muslims to return to Jerusalem
691	Dome of the Rock built in Jerusalem
950–1150	Golden Age of Spanish Jewry
1099	Crusaders capture Jerusalem
1187	Saladin recaptures Jerusalem from the Crusaders
1300s	Rise of Ottoman Muslim Dynasty in Turkey
1520–1566	Suleiman the Magnificent rules

FIRST AND SECOND ALIYAHS

1881	Start of migrations of Eastern European Jews
1882–1903	First Aliyah to Israel, mainly from Russia
1896	Theodor Herzl publishes *The Jewish State*
1897	First Zionist Congress convened by Herzl in Basel, Switzerland; World Zionist Organization founded
1904–1914	Second Aliyah, mainly from Russia and Poland
1909	First kibbutz, Degania, founded in Israel
1914–1918	World War I
1916	Start of Arab revolt against Ottoman Turkish rule
1917	Four hundred years of Ottoman rule ended by British conquest

BALFOUR DECLARATION AND MANDATORY PERIOD

1917	Balfour Declaration recognizes the right of Jews to a Jewish national home in Palestine
1919–1923	Third Aliyah, mainly from Russia
1922	Great Britain granted Mandate for Palestine by League of Nations
1922	Transjordan boundaries set
1924–1932	Fourth Aliyah, mainly from Poland
1933	Adolf Hitler becomes chancellor of Germany
1933–1939	Fifth Aliyah, mainly from Germany
1936–1939	Anti-Jewish riots instigated by Arab militants in Palestine
1939	Jewish immigration severely limited by British White Paper
1939–1945	World War II
1945	League of Arab States formed in Cairo
1947	The *Exodus 1947* sails to Palestine and is denied entry
1947	United Nations proposes the establishment of Arab and Jewish states in Palestine

THE BIRTH OF MODERN ISRAEL

1948	End of British Mandate; Declaration of Independence of the State of Israel
1948	Israel invaded by five Arab states
1948–1949	Israeli War of Independence
1948–1952	Mass immigration to Israel from Europe and Arab countries
1949	Armistice agreements signed with Egypt, Lebanon, Jordan, and Syria
1949	Jerusalem divided under Israeli and Jordanian rule
1949	First Knesset elected
1951	King Abdullah of Jordan is assassinated
1952–1954	Egyptian Republic proclaimed; Nasser takes over
1953	King Hussein officially assumes the throne in Jordan
1956	Suez War
1964	Palestine Liberation Organization (PLO) is established

SIX-DAY WAR THROUGH 1984

1967	Six-Day War
1967	UN Security Council adopts Resolution 242
1969–1970	Egypt's War of Attrition against Israel
1970	King Hussein's troops expel rebellious Palestinians backed by Syria (Black September)
1971	Hafez al-Assad seizes power in Syria
1972	Eleven Israeli athletes murdered by PLO at Munich Olympic Games
1973	Yom Kippur War
1976	Israel mounts rescue of hostages in Entebbe, Uganda
1977	Egyptian president Anwar Sadat visits Jerusalem
1978	Camp David Accords
1979	Israel-Egypt Peace Treaty signed
1981	Israeli air force destroys Iraqi nuclear reactor
1981	Egyptian president Anwar Sadat assassinated; Hosni Mubarak succeeds him
1982	Israel's three-stage withdrawal from Sinai completed
1984	Operation Moses, immigration of Jews from Ethiopia

FIRST INTIFADA THROUGH 2000

1987	First Intifada begins
1989	Start of mass immigration of Jews from former Soviet Union
1991	Israel hit by Iraqi Scud missiles during the Gulf War
1991	Operation Solomon, airlift of Jews from Ethiopia
1993	Oslo Accords signed by Israel and PLO
1994	Implementation of Palestinian self-government in Gaza Strip and Jericho area
1994	Israel-Jordan Peace Treaty signed
1994	Rabin, Peres, Arafat awarded Nobel Peace Prize
1995	Oslo II provides removal of Israeli troops from all key Palestinian towns in the West Bank
1995	Prime Minister Yitzhak Rabin assassinated at peace rally

2000 President Bill Clinton, Ehud Barak, and Yasser Arafat fail to reach agreement on Israeli-Palestinian settlement

SECOND INTIFADA THROUGH TODAY

2000 Second Intifada begins

2002 President Bush calls for Arafat to be replaced; lays out plan for a provisional Palestinian state

2005 Withdrawal from Gaza completed

2006 Hamas wins majority in Palestinian Authority general elections 2006 Hezbollah in Lebanon; month-long war begins

2007 Hamas takes over Gaza

2008 Operation Cast Lead, Israel invades Gaza

2009 Israel withdraws troops from Gaza

2009 Pope Benedict XVI visits Israel

2009 Tel Aviv centennial celebrations held

2011 "Arab Spring"

2013 Israel's population reaches eight million

2014 The PLO and Hamas form a united government; Israel suspends peace talks

2017 U.S. recognizes Jerusalem as the capital of Israel

2018 Israeli singer Netta Barzilai wins Eurovision song contest

Source: Israel Matters, Jewish Federation of Greater Los Angeles, 2015. Additional contributions by Behrman House.

Israel Today

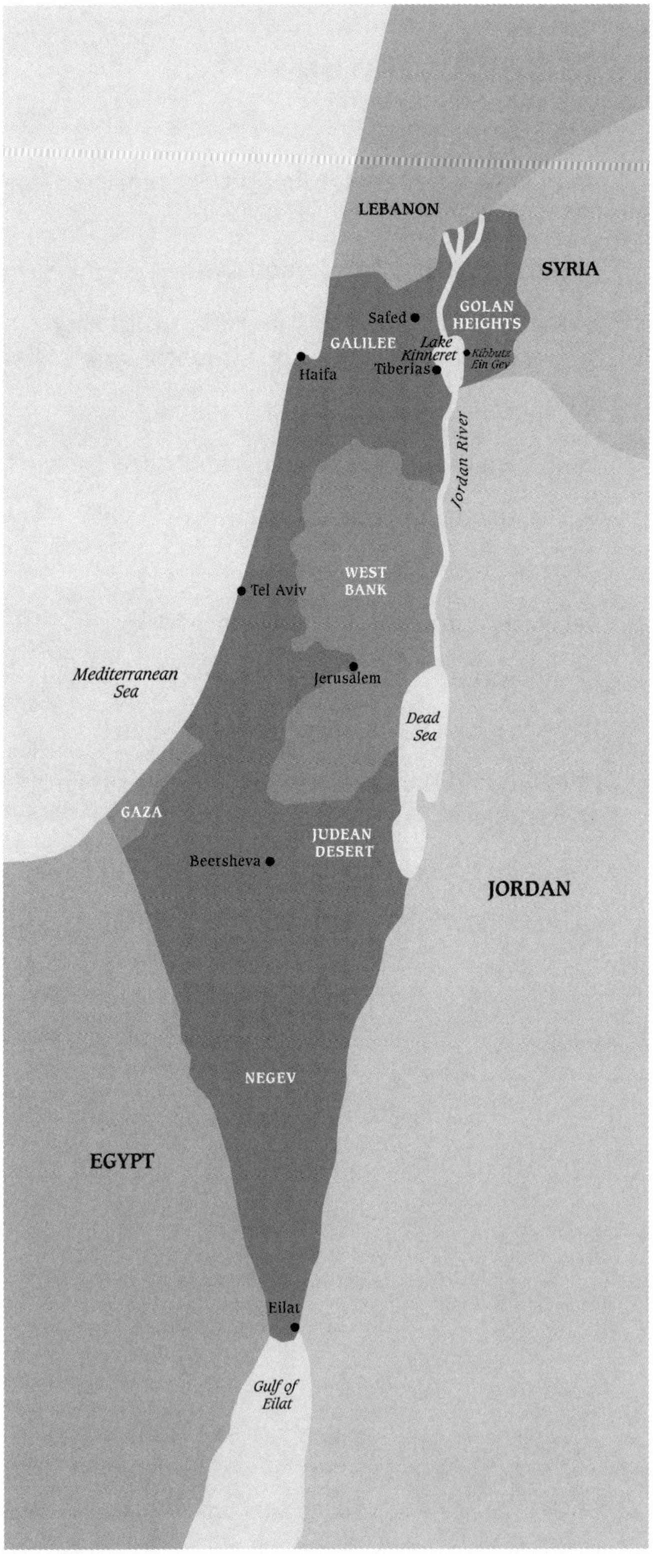

Map by Jim McMahon

Middle East Region Today

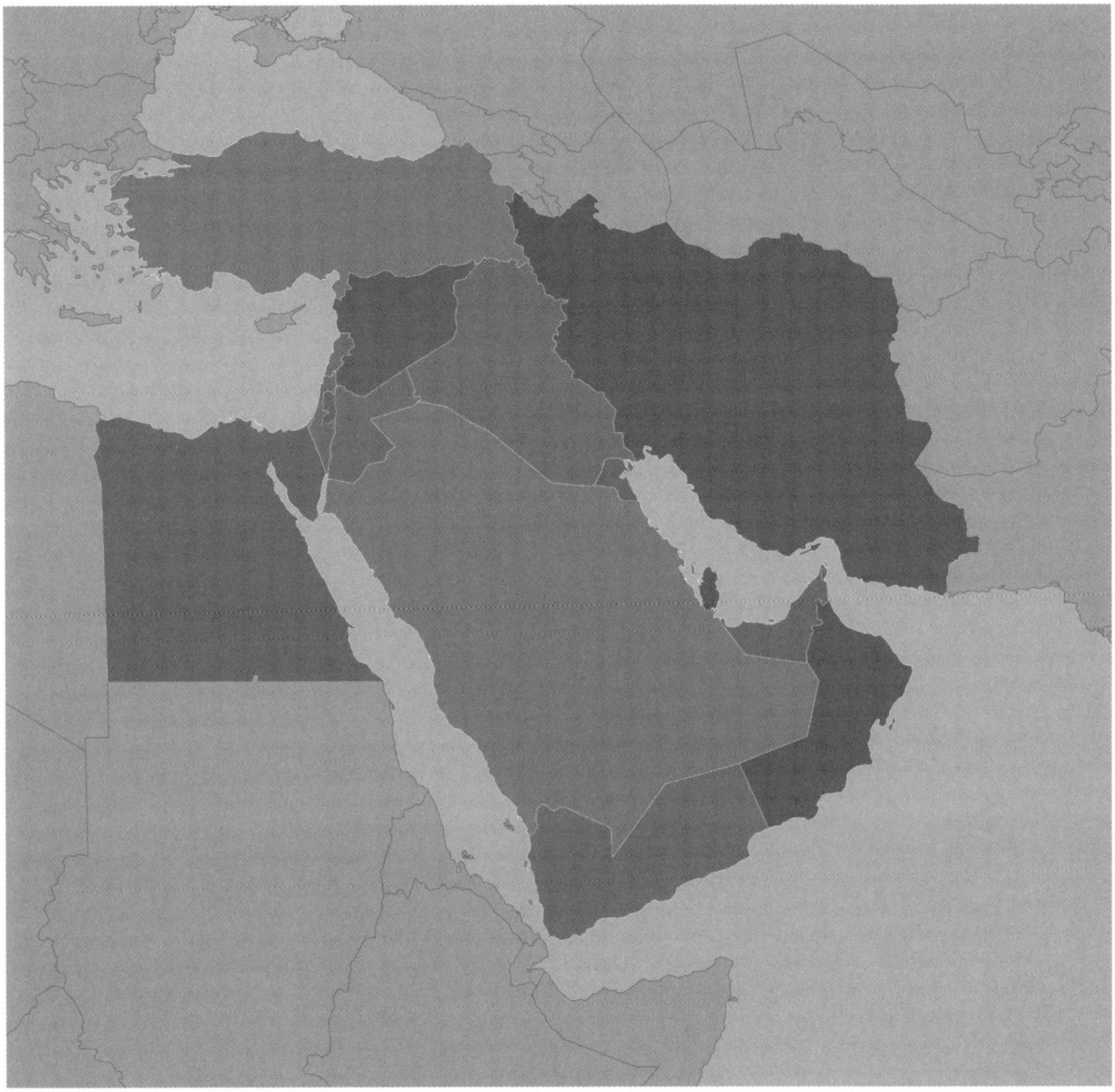

Map by Itan1409, Shutterstock

Chapter 1

It's a Home for People from All Over the World

In This Chapter

Words to Know:

***aliyah*:** literally "to go up"; refers to moving to Israel or to being called up to the Torah reading in the synagogue

Law of Return: grants every Jew the right to move to Israel and become a citizen

refuseniks: Jews in the former Soviet Union who applied to immigrate to Israel and were refused

ulpan: class designed to teach Hebrew to new immigrants to Israel

Introduction

Enduring Understanding:

People from many different ethnic, geographic, and religious backgrounds call Israel home.

Chapter Overview:

This chapter explores the meaning of a Jewish homeland and the Law of Return, which gives every Jew the right to become an Israeli citizen. Immigrants to Israel share their stories and help students understand some of the reasons people move to Israel. The Jewish value of *hachnasat orchim* (welcoming guests) guides Israelis to welcome newcomers.

Chapter 1 Lesson 1

The Jewish Homeland

Essential Question: Who are the people who call Israel home?

Learning Objectives: Students will be able to:

- Explain that Israel is home to people from all around the world.
- Describe the emotional connection many people have to Israel as the Jewish homeland.
- Articulate some of the ethical questions raised by the Law of Return.

Materials:

- "Home" by the Maccabeats **(bhlink.me/israel1)**
- crayons and/or markers (optional)

Activities

Getting Started (5 minutes)

Ask students:

> When you meet somebody for the first time, what are three or four things you'd like to know about them? Write down your questions and partner with somebody who's new to class or somebody you'd like to get to know better. Answer their questions about you, and write down their answers to your questions.

After everybody has had a chance to conduct a short "interview," ask students to introduce their partner to the rest of the class. *(Interview questions might include: Were you born here, or did you move here from somewhere else? When's your birthday? What school do you go to? What's your favorite movie, band, TV show, or book? What's your favorite sport? What's your favorite team? What's your favorite subject in school? What's your favorite Jewish holiday? What's the best vacation you've ever taken?)*

What Do You See? (5 minutes)

With a partner or in small groups, ask students to look at the pictures of Israelis at the bottom of pages 10 and 11. Then, ask them to answer the questions at the top of page 11 and jot down their interview questions to the right. When students have finished, ask them:

- What do you notice about the people in the pictures? *(their facial expressions, the variety of clothing they're wearing, the items they are holding, etc.)*
- If someone was looking at a picture of you, what might they learn about you based on your facial expression? *(You are excited, sad, serious, puzzled.)* Based on what you are wearing? *(your favorite sports team or musical group, how you dress for the weather, your favorite color)* What did you guess about the people in the photos based on what they were wearing? *(whether they're modern or traditional, how religious they might be, what ethnic background they are from, that they like sports)*
- Which person from the photos did you choose to interview? What did you want to know about that person's life? *(I'd like to know how the person feels about life in Israel; were they were born in Israel, and if not, what brought them to Israel; what is that person's religious observance like; what job does that person do?)*

The Many Flavors of Your Community (5 minutes)

Say to students:

> Just like Israeli society is diverse, so is your own Jewish community. Stand in a circle with your classmates. Imagine you are surrounding a giant salad bowl. One at a time, step into the bowl and sit down. As you do so, share what unique "flavor" you add to the community. You can include the countries your families came from, a unique tradition your family observes, or a special skill or talent you have.

Teacher Tip: Be mindful of any students who may have physical difficulty standing up or sitting on the floor for this activity. Also, be aware that some students may struggle to come up with something to say about themselves. Wherever possible, try to guide them with questions or potential answers.

Coming Home (10 minutes each)

Ask students:

- What does *home* mean to you? *(Possible answers: my house or apartment; the city, state, or country in which I live; the feeling I have when I am surrounded by my family or close friends; the place where I can freely express my emotions and thoughts.)*
- Can people have more than one place that feels like home to them? *(Possible answers: My parents are divorced, so I have two houses. Summer camp is my home away from home. I feel at home at my grandparents' house. Our vacation house in Canada, where my mom grew up, is a second home for our family.)*

After students have had a chance to share their answers with the group, choose one of the activities below. If time allows, do the other activity as well.

Activity 1: Welcome Home

Say to students:

Imagine you are writing a scene for a movie in which a character returns home after a long absence. What does that character see, feel, or hear? Write the dialogue for that scene in the space on pages 12 and 13 in your book. When you are done, trade scripts with a partner and review them. Then, discuss the following questions:

- What did the scripts you and your partner wrote have in common? What was different? *(Scripts may include some similar or some very different characters; scripts may include very similar or very different ideas or emotions attached to coming home.)*
- What emotions did the characters in both scripts feel? *(Characters may be happy, relieved, angry, hurt, loved, etc.)*

Activity 2: The Maccabeats Go Home

Tell students that the Maccabeats are a Jewish singing group. Play the video of their song "Home" **(bhlink.me/israel1)**. Then, ask students, in groups of three or four, to answer the following questions:

- What do you think the Maccabeats are feeling when they are in Israel? Why do you think they feel that way? *(They are happy when they're in Israel; they feel connected and at home. They share the feeling of many Jews around the world that Israel is the Jewish homeland. They think about and miss Israel even when they're home in New York City.)*
- If you also completed Activity 1, what emotions did the Maccabeats share with your script characters? *(happiness, connection, comfort, etc.)*
- Now that you've thought more about what home means, what does the idea of a Jewish homeland mean to you? *(It's a place where Jews are always welcomed, a place where most people will understand your values and traditions, a place where you share history with other Jews.)*

Building Activity: Home Away from Home

Hand out crayons/markers and paper to students and say:

Think of two places that feel like home to you, and draw a picture of them. How are the places similar? How are they different? Are they related to each other in some way? Using words or emojis, describe how each place makes you feel.

What If You're Not Jewish? (15 minutes)

Randomly divide students into pairs. You may also wish to split the group into two teams. Tell them that they're going to debate the Law of Return, which is explained in "The Jewish Homeland" on page 12 of their books: Yes, it's a thoughtful policy, or No, it's an unfair policy. Assure students that it's okay if they don't necessarily agree with the side they are presenting.

Read the following aloud to students:

The Law of Return grants you the right to move to Israel and become a citizen if you're Jewish or have a Jewish family member, such as a grandparent, parent, or spouse. Others can apply to become a permanent resident or citizen of Israel.

Ask those on the "Yes" side to list on page 13 of the student book several reasons why they think the Law of Return is a fair policy. Ask those on the "No" side to list reasons why the Law of Return is unfair. Partners or teams should debate with each other.

After the debate, ask students:

- What points did your partner or the other team make?
- What points did you or your team make?
- After listening to your partner or the other team, has your position changed? If yes, how? If not, why not?

(Here are some potential arguments for and against:

***YES:** As a Jewish state, it makes sense that Israel would give citizenship priority to Jews. As Jews continue to face discrimination around the world, Israel has an obligation to be a safe haven for Jews. Other people are welcome, but that doesn't mean they need to be a priority.*

***NO:** It goes against the Jewish value of hachnasat orchim, "welcoming guests" and including the stranger, to grant automatic citizenship only to Jews. It is discriminatory, which is especially disappointing given how Jews have been harmed by discriminatory policies in other countries.)*

Teacher Tip: Note that we will return to the ethical questions raised by the Law of Return later in this chapter.

Feels Like Home (5 minutes)

Ask students:

Name five things about Israel that makes it feel like home to so many Jews around the world. *(Potential answers include: our long history in the land, being surrounded by other Jews, hearing and speaking Hebrew, Jewish holiday supplies being featured and readily available at stores and markets, visiting holy sites like the Kotel, etc.)*

How do you feel about Israel? Does it feel like a home away from home to you? Why or why not? *(Some students may have that connection to Israel; others may not. It may depend on whether they've visited Israel, what they believe about Israel, or what home means to them.)*

Chapter 1 Lesson 2
The People Who Come

Essential Question: Why do people move to Israel, and how does Israel welcome new immigrants?

Learning Objectives: Students will be able to:

- Explain what leads people to move to Israel.
- Articulate challenges that immigrants face once in Israel.
- Discuss the needs of new immigrants and the steps Israel has taken to meet those needs.

Materials:

- blank paper, large sticky notes, or kraft paper
- markers or crayons
- T'filat Haderech text (**bhlink.me/israel1**; or you may wish to print out copies for students)
- "T'filat Haderech" by Debbie Friedman (**bhlink.me/israel1**; optional)
- "Just Another Foreigner" by Safam (**bhlink.me/israel1**; optional)
- magazines or printed pictures of household items (optional)
- scissors or tape (optional)

Activities

Getting Started (5 minutes)

Write the following questions on the board as students arrive, and ask them to jot down their answers.

- Why do you think someone might want to move to Israel? *(Possible answers might include: Because they are Zionists, because they want to live in a place with lots of other Jews, because they want better opportunities, because life in their home country is no longer safe.)*
- Where do you think immigrants to Israel come from? *(anywhere or everywhere in the world)*
- What challenges might immigrants face when they get to Israel? *(language barriers, finding a job, discrimination, securing housing, making new friends, adjusting to a new school)*

The People Who Come (15 Minutes)

Divide the class into four groups. Assign each group one of the immigrants on pages 14 through 17: Karen, Roman, Esther, or Marc. Ask each group to read their immigrant's story and consider the following questions:

- What stood out to you about this story? What was especially interesting or surprising? *(Answers may include: how hard it is for Karen to learn Hebrew, how the Soviet government treated Roman's family, the dangers Ethiopian Jews faced on their journey, the challenges Ethiopians faced in adjusting to modern technology, that Marc's dad lives part time in France and part time in Israel).*
- If you could meet one of these immigrants, what would you want to ask him or her? *(What led your family to move? What is life really like in Israel? What was life like in the country where you or your family came from? What economic factors influence how families live in Israel?)*
- Karen was a Jewish kid living in North America, probably a lot like you. How would you feel if your family decided to make *aliyah? (Emotions may include: excited, nervous, hopeful, sad. Students may have specific concerns about what it might be like to move there, how hard it might be to leave their friends behind, or they might be curious about attending an Israeli school.)*

After the groups have discussed these questions, tell them that they are going to hold an "Immigrant Summit." One person from each group will represent the immigrant they just learned about. In preparation, each group will create a backdrop on kraft paper representing their immigrant. They might include symbols, such as a flag, of the country from which their immigrant emigrated; "photos" of family members, a map showing the immigrant's journey to Israel, etc. Hang the backdrops on the wall behind the panel. Choose one student to be the moderator. The rest of the students are the reporters. Have the immigrants present their stories from the front of the room. Have the moderator call on the reporters one at a time to pose questions to the immigrants. The questions can include some of the discussion topics above.

The Blessing of Making Aliyah (10 minutes)

Say to students:

> In Jewish tradition, we say T'filat Haderech, the Traveler's Prayer, before embarking on a journey. What prayer would you offer to people about to make aliyah? Read the text of T'filat Haderech **(bhlink.me/israel1)**, then, with a partner, write your prayer on a sheet of paper.

You may wish to play Debbie Friedman's song, "T'filat Haderech" **(bhlink.me/israel1)** for inspiration.

Building Activity: Just Another Foreigner

Play the song "Just Another Foreigner" by Safam. You can also read the lyrics at **bhlink.me/israel1**. *Falasha* was a term used to describe Ethiopian Jews. It is now considered derogatory but wasn't at the time this song was written. Many people now call this group Beta Israel, the House of Israel.

Ask students:

How do the stories in this song compare to those of Roman and Esther? How did you feel while listening to this song? *(The singers focus on how, even though we might look different, we are all one Jewish family. The woman in Odessa has not yet made it to Israel. She might represent some of the family and friends Roman's family left behind.)*

Welcoming the New Arrivals (15 minutes)

Ask a volunteer to read "Welcoming the New Arrivals" at the bottom of page 18. Then ask:

Imagine you have just moved to a new country. What kinds of things might you need? What would help you get settled in your new home? Let's imagine what Karen, Roman, Esther, and Marc's families might have wished for when they immigrated to Israel.

Write answers on the board or on a large sheet of paper taped to the wall.

Divide students into four groups, one for each of the families they read about, and distribute art supplies (and magazines or printed pictures of household items, if you've decided to include them). Have students create a drawing or collage of the welcome package they'd make, including the supplies they thought of above, on page 19 of their books (or on blank paper or kraft paper, if you prefer). Then, invite students to share their artwork with the class and answer these questions:

- Why did you choose each item? *(I knew they would need supplies for cooking, to help kids feel safe in their new rooms, to help them learn Hebrew, to keep them warm in the winter, etc.)*
- How do you imagine each item would help the family you selected feel welcome? *(help them create a home, help them adjust to their new country, help kids to deal with the transition, provide a way for them to welcome guests and make new friends)*

Building Activity: Welcome to the Neighborhood

Activity 1: Welcome Basket

As a class social action project, consider making a welcome package or two for new immigrants to your community. Check with your local Jewish Family Service, or a local refugee or immigrant resettlement program, to ask what new arrivals need. Items may include dishes, silverware, sheets, pillows, stuffed animals, books, cleaning supplies. Most places request that items be new or in very good condition. Invite parents to bring donations to class, and to help pack and deliver the welcome basket(s). Make a welcome card from the entire class to accompany the package.

Activity 2: Immigration History

Encourage students to speak with their parents or grandparents about the immigration history of their own family. When did their family come here? Where did they emigrate from? Why? Invite students to share what they learned the next time you meet.

Teacher Tip: You may wish to send home an email with instructions about Activity 2. Sample text below:

> Dear Parents,
>
> In class, we have been learning about immigrants to Israel. To better understand these immigrants, I would like students to explore their families' own immigration histories. Students have been asked to interview you and/or your parents (or other family members). Questions to ask might include:
>
> - When did our family come here?
> - Where did they emigrate from?
> - Why did they emigrate?
> - What were their first impressions of life here?
>
> If this is not a topic you feel comfortable discussing, please encourage your child to interview a family friend or neighbor instead. Please help students record the answers to their questions and bring them to school. Students will be asked to share what they have learned with the class the next time we meet.

Teacher Tip: To create further excitement, students could dress in period costume and present to the class as their relative. Or, students could bring in objects or photos that have personal meaning or relevance to their family's country of emigration. If you decide to offer these options, be sure to add instructions to the e-mail you send to parents.

Teacher Tip: Some students or families may have complicated immigration histories. Students who were adopted may feel uncomfortable if they don't know the history of their birth parents. Students who have insecure immigration status may be scared to share personal information. If you are concerned, give the option of interviewing family friends or neighbors who may have interesting immigration stories to share as modeled in the sample email to parents.

Chapter 1 Lesson 3

Who Is a Jew? It's Complicated

Essential Question: How does someone prove they are Jewish to make *aliyah* under the Law of Return?

Learning Objectives: Students will be able to:

- List some of the many ways people identify as Jewish.
- Identify the challenges of having to prove Jewish identity to make *aliyah.*
- Explain the perspectives of both the Israeli government and potential immigrants about the *aliyah* process.

Activities

Who Is a Jew? (10 minutes)

Invite a volunteer to read "Who Is a Jew?" at the top of page 20.

Ask students:

How would you feel if someone asked you to prove that you are Jewish? *(Possible answers might include: frustration at not being trusted, concern that I am not "Jewish enough" to meet government standards; proud and happy to share my background.)*

Ask for two other volunteers, one to read aloud "But What Makes Someone Jewish?" and one to read "What Does the Jewish State Do?" (also on page 20). Ask students to answer the following questions with a partner.

- Why do you think the Israeli government has rules about proving Jewishness?
- Is this a good or bad idea, and why? (*As a Jewish state, the government wants to ensure that the needs of Jews are given priority in the immigration process; there are many rules in Israel affecting Jews that depend on Jewish status, such as the ability of Jews to get married in Israel. Others might argue that we have an obligation to help others, whether or not they are Jewish.)*

Getting Your Driver's License (5 minutes)

Before completing the next activity, it will be helpful for students to understand the idea of documentation. Using computers or cell phones, ask students to go to the website for the Department of Motor Vehicles in your state. Say:

> Imagine you are preparing to apply for a driver's license. What documentation would you need to bring with you to the Department of Motor Vehicles?

List their findings on the board. Then ask:

> If somebody asked you to prove you are Jewish, what kind of documents could you present as proof?

Write their answers to this question on the board. Keep the list posted as they complete the following activity.

Proving Jewishness (20 minutes)

Have students pair up. One student will play an immigrant who is hoping to become an Israeli citizen under the Law of Return. The other will play an Israeli government official who is conducting the interview to determine whether the immigrant can make *aliyah*. Before you begin, the person playing the immigrant should decide which country he or she is from and what his or her Jewish connection is. Students can use the table on page 21 of their books to document their role play.

(Possible questions from the government official might include:

- *Were any of your great-grandparents Jewish? If so, what evidence do you have?*
- *Do you have a document, like a bar or bat mitzvah certificate, that shows your ongoing Jewish practice?*
- *What objects do you have in your home that can prove your commitment to Jewish practice?*
- *Do you have a relationship with your community rabbi? Would your rabbi be willing to testify that your family is Jewish?*
- *Do you have a copy of your parents' ketubah (Jewish wedding contract)?*
- *What Jewish education, if any, have you received?*
- *Do you have a certificate from your brit (circumcision) or simchat bat (ceremony to welcome Jewish girls into the Covenant)?*
- *Can you read or speak Hebrew?*
- *Can you recite the Mah Nishtanah (Four Questions at the Passover seder)?*
- *If you converted, do you have the necessary paperwork? Who conducted your conversion? Same questions apply if your mother converted.*
- *Do you have a passport from your home country? Does it indicate your religion?*
- *Are you married to someone who is Jewish?*
- *Do you have a picture of the gravestone of an ancestor that was Jewish? How are you related?*

The answers to these questions will obviously vary depending on the stories students have created for this activity. Potential challenges the immigrant might face include:

- *Parents lived somewhere where a Jewish wedding wasn't possible or the k'tubah had to be left behind when fleeing a dangerous situation.*
- *Immigrant may have lived somewhere where it wasn't safe to get a Jewish education. Or, the government official might feel the education wasn't rigorous enough.*
- *Immigrant may not have a relationship with a rabbi.*
- *Immigrant's parents may not have had the option or the resources for a brit, simchat bat, or bar/ bat mitzvah.*
- *Immigrant may not have enough Jewish education to speak Hebrew or know the Mah Nishtanah.)*

After they have completed their role play, ask students:

- How did it feel to be the government official? *(like I was interrogating someone who had done nothing wrong, frustrating to follow rules I may not personally agree with, proud to be a part of the process allowing people to make aliyah)*
- How did it feel to be the immigrant? *(like I wasn't trusted that I am who I say I am, like my Judaism isn't "valid" enough, still excited at the prospect of moving to Israel)*

Building Activity: Immigration History

If you assigned the Building Activity called "Immigration History" in the previous lesson, ask students to share their relatives' stories. If you've asked students to dress in costume or bring in personal objects or photos, give them a few additional minutes to prepare. Here are some of the questions students might have discussed with close family members:

- When did our family come here?
- Where did they emigrate from?
- Why did they emigrate?
- What were their first impressions of life here?

Mark a world map or do a tally on the board showing the countries from which students' families emigrated. Discuss the reasons why they emigrated, and compare their reasons to those that students learned from "The People Who Come" on pages 14 through 17 in their books. *(Family members might have emigrated for greater economic opportunities, to join family members who had emigrated earlier, because of war, anti-Semitism, for medical assistance, etc. Among the reasons in their book that Karen, Roman, Esther, and Marc or their families emigrated are Zionism/religious beliefs, persecution/anti-Semitism, economic considerations, and famine.)*

Building Activity: Invite an Immigrant

Has someone in your community immigrated to your town or city from another country? Do you know someone who has made *aliyah*? Invite them to speak to your class about their own experiences, either in person or via video chat. Ask the education director, clergy, or Jewish Federation for suggestions of whom to contact.

Reflections: Talk about It! (10 minutes)

Discuss these three questions as a group:

1. Compare the different types of immigrant experiences that you learned about. In what ways were they similar? Different?*(Immigrants came from many different countries and spoke different languages. Many immigrants faced some challenges when they arrived in Israel as they acclimated to their new home. Some had an easier time than others adjusting to their new homes.)*
2. Which of the stories on pages 14 through 17 did you connect with the most? *(When I read about the immigrants, I felt compassion for them: the challenges some of the immigrants faced were very difficult, they were nervous about moving to a new country. Their stories reminded me of stories I have heard in my own family. I related to Karen's story because her life is most similar to mine.)*
3. Why do you think people from around the world choose to immigrate to Israel? *(Some immigrants came because of their love for Israel, a belief in Zionism, or a strong Jewish identity, while others came to escape anti-Semitism or challenging living conditions elsewhere. Some may have come to be closer to family or friends who are already in Israel.)*

Additional Resources

The following activities and information can supplement the lessons or be used on their own to enrich learning about Israel as a home for people from all over the world.

First Day in the *Merkaz K'litah:* An Activity About Home

By Marc Rosenstein

In this activity, you will simulate the welcoming reception for a group of new families arriving at an absorption center *(merkaz k'litah)*. Groups of students will play the roles of families from different countries of origin. You could invite parents or older students to join you for the simulation. This activity has the potential to be much more elaborate, with students coming prepared with costumes, photos or other props.

- Introduce the concept of home by having students tell each other about their homes and share what is important to them about their home. Does "home" mean the same thing as "house?"
- Tell students that they are part of a family that decided to move to Israel and they have just arrived at a hostel for new families, the *merkaz k'litah,* where they will live for a few months in a small apartment until they get settled. Their neighbors are families from other places around the world. They are at the welcome party the center is holding for all new arrivals. Divide the group into small groups of three to five students. Assign each an Identity Card (see following page).
- Give each group a few minutes to read over their assigned card and decide who will play what role in the family (parent, child, grandparent). Have them consider the following questions:

1 What language do you speak? What's it like in the land you came from?

2 Why did you decide to leave your come and come live in Israel?

3 What about Israel (the land, climate, etc.) reminds you of the land you left behind? What's the biggest difference?

4 What will you miss most about the place you left behind?

5 What are you most happy to leave behind?

6 What are you worried about in Israel?

7 What are you looking forward to in Israel?

- Assemble the full group in a circle with families sitting together. You are the social director and allow each group to introduce themselves. Give each family a few chances to speak, rather than long presentations from each group. Have each family point out their country of origin on a world map. Use questions to help students imagine the experience of immigration, the motivation of Jews from various places to uproot and move to Israel, and the "costs" (finding a new job, being isolated from friends and family who stayed behind, learning a new language, new foods, feeling different, etc.) and "benefits" (finding Jewish friends, being in a secure majority, escaping anti-Semitism, etc.) of such a decision for different family members.
- After each family has shared its experience, discuss the language problem. Ask them how, in real life, they would be able to have this party. Consider having the families communicate using only the Hebrew they know and sign language. Hebrew is a binding force among Jews from all corners.
- Have students step out of their roles and discuss: What do these very different Jews have in common? *(Jewish holidays, Shabbat, Hebrew, belief in God, love of Israel, history)*
- Write *Am Yisrael Chai* on the board. Ask the students to step back into their roles at the absorption center party. Sing the song together as a group to celebrate their new friends and new home.

Source: From *CHAI Israel Strand Curriculum Core*, URJ Press

Identity Cards

Country: Russia

Language spoken in original country: Russian. Many older individuals also spoke Yiddish.

How to say "hello" in this language: Privyet

Location: Eastern Europe and Northern Asia

Climate and geography: Russia is the biggest country in the world. There is a wide variation of climate and landscape, including glaciers, deserts, mountains, and plains.

Traditional food from this country: Borscht (beet soup)

Jewish population in this country: 179,500

Background on Jewish life in this country: Jews migrated to modern-day Russian in the Middle Ages. In the late 1800s, Jews were badly persecuted, and many fled to other countries. In the 20th century, the Communist government there persecuted Jews but would not allow them to leave Russia. Since 1991, when the Communist government ended, many Jews have left Russia for Israel, the United States, Europe, and Canada.

Country: *Iraq*

Language spoken in original country: *Arabic*

How to say "hello" in this language: *Marhaba*

Location: *The Middle East*

Climate and geography: *Iraq is mainly composed of desert with some farmland and mountains*

Traditional food from this country: *Kubeh (dumplings filled with meat)*

Jewish population in this country: *Fewer than 100*

Background on Jewish life in this country: *Abraham was born in a city in modern-day Iraq. After the First Temple was destroyed in Jerusalem more than 2,500 years ago, many Jews were taken captive to Babylonia (modern-day Iraq). Jews have lived there ever since. After the establishment of the State of Israel n 1948, most Iraqi Jews emigrated.*

Country: *Argentina*

Language spoken in original country: *Spanish*

How to say "hello" in this language: *Buenos dias*

Location: *South America*

Climate and geography: *Argentina includes huge wide, flat plains; mountains, big rivers, and a long seacoast. Summers are hot.*

Traditional food from this country: *Carne asado (roasted meat)*

Jewish population in this country: *184,500*

Background on Jewish life in this country: *Large populations of Jews started moving to Argentina in the 1800s. Jews there have sometimes suffered persecution. There is a large, well-educated community in Argentina, but in recent decades many Jews have immigrated to the United States and Israel.*

Country: *United States*

Language spoken in original country: *English*

Location: *North America*

Climate and geography: *There is wide variation of climate and landscape, including glaciers, deserts, forests, mountains, and plains.*

Traditional ethnic food from this country: *Bagels*

Jewish population in this country: *5,275,000*

Background on Jewish life in this country: *Jews first came to North America in 1654. Ever since, there have been waves of Jewish immigration to the United States from all over the world.*

Country: *India*

Language spoken in original country: *Hindi and English*

How to say "hello" in this language: *Nah-mas-tay (Hindi)*

Location: *South Asia*

Climate and geography: *India is composed of mountains, jungles, deserts, and a long coastline. Northern India is warm, and southern India enjoys a tropical climate.*

Traditional ethnic food from this country: *Mango chutney*

Jewish population in this country: *5,000*

Background on Jewish life in this country: *It is unclear when Jews first moved to India, but it was centuries ago. A Jewish population grew as India was ruled by England in the 18th and early 19th centuries. Since the 1940s, many Indian Jews have moved to Israel, the United States, and England.*

The Law of Return

The Law of Return 5710 (1950)*

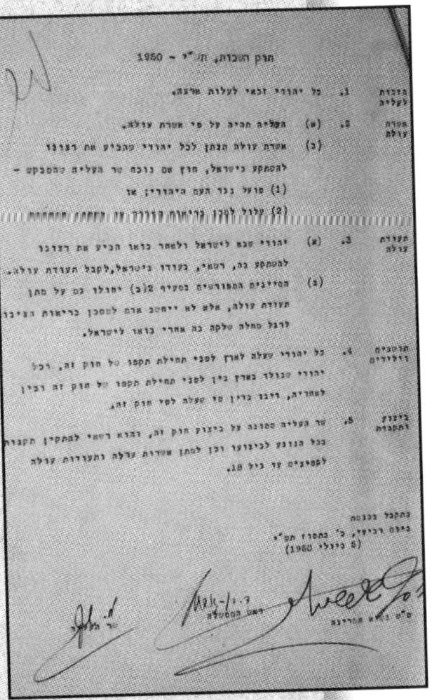

1 Every Jew has the right to come to this country as an oleh**.

2 (a) Aliyah shall be by oleh's visa.

(b) An oleh's visa shall be granted to every Jew who has expressed his desire to settle in Israel, unless the Minister of Immigration is satisfied that the applicant

(1) is engaged in an activity directed against the Jewish people; or

(2) is likely to endanger public health or the security of the State.

3 (a) A Jew who has come to Israel and subsequent to his arrival has expressed his desire to settle in Israel may, while still in Israel, receive an oleh's certificate.

(b) The restrictions specified in section 2(b) shall apply also to the grant of an oleh's certificate, but a person shall not be regarded as endangering public health on account of an illness contracted after his arrival in Israel.

4 Every Jew who has immigrated into this country before the coming into force of this Law, and every Jew who was born in this country, whether before or after the coming into force of this Law, shall be deemed to be a person who has come to this country as an oleh under this Law.

5 The Minister of Immigration is charged with the implementation of this Law and may make regulations as to any matter relating to such implementation and also as to the grant of an oleh's visas and oleh's certificate to minors up to the age of 18 years.

DAVID BEN-GURION *Prime Minister*	*MOSHE SHAPIRA* *Minister of Immigration*	*YOSEF SPRINZAK* *Acting President of the State* *Chairman of the Knesset*

* Passed by the Knesset on the 20th Tammuz, 5710 (5th July, 1950)
** Translator's Note: *Aliyah* means immigration of Jews, and *oleh* (plural: *olim*) means a Jew immigrating, into Israel.

Source: The State of Israel, knesset.gov

Law of Return, Amendment 5714 (1954)*

Amendment of section 2(b)

1. In section 2 (b) of the Law of Return, 5710–1950 -

(1) the full stop at the end of paragraph (2) shall be replaced by a semi-colon, and the word "or" shall be inserted thereafter ;

(2) the following paragraph shall be inserted after paragraph (2):

"(3) is a person with a criminal past, likely to endanger public welfare."

Amendment of sections 2 and 5

2. In sections 2 and 5 of the Law, the words "the Minister of Immigration" shall be replaced by the words "the Minister of the Interior".

* Passed by the Knesset on the 24th Av, 5714 (23rd August, 1954)

Source: The State of Israel, knesset.gov

Law of Return, Amendment No. 2 5730 (1970)*

Addition of sections 4A and 4B

1. In the Law of Return, 5710-1950, the following sections shall be inserted after section 4:

"Rights of members of family

4A. (a) The rights of a Jew under this Law and the rights of an oleh under the Nationality Law, 5712-1952, as well as the rights of an oleh under any other enactment, are also vested in a child and a grandchild of a Jew, the spouse of a Jew, the spouse of a child of a Jew and the spouse of a grandchild of a Jew, except for a person who has been a Jew and has voluntarily changed his religion.

(b) It shall be immaterial whether or not a Jew by whose right a right under subsection (a) is claimed is still alive and whether or not he has immigrated to Israel.

(c) The restrictions and conditions prescribed in respect of a Jew or an oleh by or under this Law or by the enactments referred to in subsection (a) shall also apply to a person who claims a right under subsection (a).

Definition

4B. For the purposes of this Law, "Jew" means a person who was born of a Jewish mother or has become converted to Judaism and who is not a member of another religion."

Amendment of section 5

2. In section 5 of the Law of Return, 5710-1950, the following shall be added at the end: "Regulations for the purposes of sections 4A and 4B require the approval of the Constitution, Legislation and Juridical Committee of the Knesset."

Amendment of the Population Registry Law, 5725-1965

3. In the Population Registry Law, 5725-1965, the following section shall be inserted after section 3:

"Power of registration and definition

3A. (a) A person shall not be registered as a Jew by ethnic affiliation or religion if a notification under this Law or another entry in the Registry or a public document indicates that he is not a Jew, so long as the said notification, entry or document has not been controverted to the satisfaction of the Chief Registration Officer or so long as declaratory judgment of a competent court or tribunal has not otherwise determined.

(b) For the purposes of this Law and of any registration or document thereunder, "Jew" has the same meaning as in section 4B of the Law of Return, 5710-1950.

(c) This section shall not derogate from a registration effected before its coming into force."

GOLDA MEIR
Prime Minister
Acting Minister of the Interior

SHNEUR ZALMAN SHAZAR
President of the State

* Passed by the Knesset on 2nd Adar Bet, 5730 (10th March, 1970)

Source: The State of Israel, knesset.gov

By the Numbers

Jewish Immigration to Palestine and United States 1881-1928

Years	Palestine	United States
1881-1903	25,000	861,103
1904-1914	40,000	1,194,497
1919-1923	35,000	236,571
1924-1928	67,000	43,681
TOTALS	**167,000**	**2,335,852**

Sources: Immigration to Palestine: Jewish Agency for Israel, www.jewishagency.org/historical-aliyah/content/28841
Immigration to the United States: American Jewish Year Book 77 (1977), p. 319

By the Numbers

Immigration to Israel, by Country of Origin 1948–1951

Country	Number of Immigrants	Country	Number of Immigrants
Iraq	123,371	Afghanistan	2,303
Romania	117,950	India	2,176
Poland	106,414	Greece	2,131
Yemen	48,315	United Kingdom	1,907
Bulgaria	37,260	United States	1,711
Turkey	34,547	Netherlands	1,077
Libya	30,792	Italy	1,035
Morocco	28,263	Argentina	904
Iran	21,910	South Africa	666
Czechoslovakia	18,788	China	504
Egypt, Sudan	16,024	Brazil	304
Hungary	14,324	Canada	236
Tunisia	13,293	Lebanon	235
Germany	8,210	Switzerland	131
USSR (Ukraine/Russia)	8,163	Australia, New Zealand	119
Yugoslavia	7,661	Spain	80
Algeria	3,810	Uruguay	66
France	3,050	Mexico	48
Syria	2,678	Chile	48
Austria	2,632	Ethiopia	10

Source: Israel Central Bureau of Statistics

Chapter 2

It's a Mix of Cultures

In This Chapter

Words to Know:

***chag samei'ach*:** happy holidays

***hamantashen*:** triangle—shaped cookies eaten on Purim, designed to imitate the corners of Haman's hat; also called *oznei Haman* (Haman's ears)

***sufganiyot*:** jelly donuts, often served on Hanukkah

Introduction

Enduring Understanding:

Israeli culture is a blend of many influences—ancient and modern, and Jewish, Arab, and Western.

Chapter Overview:

This chapter explores how Israeli life is influenced by cultures from around the world, and how ancient and historical figures and places are part of modern daily life. Everything in Israel—from street signs to food to music—is shaped by these different cultures. Israelis benefit from diversity, though they are sometimes divided by their differences.

Chapter 2 Lesson 1

Jewish, Arab, and Western Culture

Essential Question: How do Jewish, Arab, and Western influences shape modern Israeli culture?

Learning Objectives: Students will be able to:

- Identify differences in how Jewish holidays are celebrated in Israel and outside of Israel.
- Cite examples of how Jewish historical figures are commemorated in modern ways.
- Explain how the Arabic language and Arab food and music are part of Israeli daily life.
- Recognize that many of their own cultural interests, including sports, books, music, and movies, are also popular parts of Israeli life.

Materials:

- crayons or markers
- glue
- scissors
- holiday videos (bhlink.me/israel2)
- Machane Yehuda Street Art videos (bhlink.me/israel2)
- printouts of Israeli graffiti paintings from the Machane Yehuda street market in Jerusalem
- colored paper (optional)
- T-shirts and fabric markers/paints (optional)

Activities

Getting Started (5 minutes)

In small groups, ask students to imagine a family with children their age visiting our country for the first time. If students could take their guests to see three places, what places would they choose? A historic site? A sports game? A restaurant? What would it feel like to visit those places? What would those places help visitors understand about our country and the people who live in it?

What Do You See? (5 minutes)

Ask students, working in pairs, to look at the pictures from Israel found on pages 22 and 23 and discuss the questions. When students are finished, ask them to share their answers with the class:

- What words or ideas come to mind when looking at these photos? *(Answers may include: beautiful, colorful, diversity, food, gathering places, Israelis.)*
- Several of the photos show examples of food. Why do you think food plays such an important role in culture? *(The concept of "breaking bread" has always encouraged people to build relationships over meals; good food is something everyone can appreciate; part of the joy of traveling is sampling new cuisines, etc.)*

The Jewish Connection (10 minutes each)

Pick one of the activities below, or, if time permits, do both. Each of these activities connects Jewish holidays or history to modern life.

Activity 1: Compare: Holidays Here, Holidays There

Step 1: In the top box (page 23), ask students to draw or glue images that describe how they celebrate Jewish holidays in their neighborhood or synagogue. *(Pictures may include apples and honey, a religious school class decorating a sukkah, a dreidel, a family gathered at a seder.)*

Step 2: Based on the holidays students have chosen, show videos **(bhlink.me/israel2)** about how those holidays are celebrated in Israel.

Step 3: Ask students to create an image in the second box that describes how Israelis celebrate that same Jewish holiday.

Step 4: Ask students to compare the two celebrations. What do they have in common? How are they different? What was surprising to them?

(Core traditions may be similar, but details may change. For example, the letters on dreidels in Israel stand for the words "a great miracle happened here," while the letters on dreidels outside of Israel stand for the words "a great miracle happened there"; Israelis eat sufganiyot instead of/in addition to latkes for Hanukkah; the length of holidays outside of Israel may be longer than in Israel; the scale of holiday celebrations, like Purim parades or the easy availability of kosher-for-Passover food, may be larger in Israel since there are more people celebrating.)

Activity 2: Design: Heroic Street Art

Watch the video at **bhlink.me/Israel 2** to see a series of paintings from the Machane Yehuda street market in Jerusalem that brings Jewish heroes to life. Then, ask each student to choose one of the printouts you have made of one of the heroes depicted in the graffiti paintings and paste the picture in the space provided on page 25 of their book.

Students should then go online or look in the library and find out five key facts about that person. Adding their own words and drawings on top and around the printed image of the heroes students have chosen, they can express their connections to these people and how they feel about them. If time permits, encourage students who wish to do so to share their work with the class.

Teacher Tip: This activity can be done in small groups. The printouts, with students' words and drawings, can be mounted on colored paper and hung in the classroom.

Building Activity: Where Did It Come From?

Ask students if they can think of examples of words from other languages that are part of their vocabulary. How do they think those words became part of the English language? What can that teach us about how languages evolve?

(If students can't think of examples, provide some for them:

- *Yiddish: shvitz=sweat, nosh=eat, shlep=carry, klutz=a clumsy person*
- *French: bon appétit!=good appetite, buffet=an arrangement of food from which people can serve themselves, café=a small restaurant*
- *Spanish: foods like tacos and nachos, siesta=nap)*

Arabic Culture: Have a Chat (5 minutes)

Have students read page 26 in their books and practice using Arabic words in "Have a Chat." Then ask them to share their funniest sentences with the class.

Make Some Music (10 minutes)

In small groups, have students listen to the songs at bhlink.me/israel2 or choose a song they all like a lot. Then have them develop movements that highlight the most important lyrics from the song; for example, maybe the group stomps or waves their hands in the air when an important word is said.

Still in their groups, have students discuss the following questions:

- Have you ever connected with someone over a favorite song or band? Share why you think music might help bring people together. *(Listening to music together, whether at a concert or recorded, is a shared emotional experience; discussions about music and musicians can provide common ground for people who may not have much else in common.)*
- What can music tell you about culture or community? *(Music can highlight historical connections, modern issues, influences of other groups, political passions, etc.)*
- How can music help people in minority communities share their culture with others? *(Music can be a safe way to transmit powerful ideas, address social justice issues like racism and oppression, and bring people together both in celebration and in grief. It provides an outlet for disenfranchised people to have a voice.)*

Ask each group to perform their song and movement for the class.

Western Culture: Design Your T-Shirt (10 minutes)

Invite volunteers to read page 28 aloud. Then encourage students to look at the pictures of clothing found on page 29 of their books. Ask:

Do you recognize any of the things featured in the clothing here? *(Students might recognize sports teams like the Boston Red Sox or the Toronto Blue Jays.)*

Say:

Israeli kids wear clothes that highlight some of the same things that your clothes do. In the space on page 29 of your books, design your own T-shirt using Hebrew letters to honor your favorite band, sports team, movie, or book.

Encourage students to share their designs with the class. Ask:

How does your T-shirt design make you feel connected to Israeli kids your age? *(Knowing that we're fans of some of the same sports teams, movies, music, and books means that we'd have things to talk about if we were to meet. Sharing some interests probably means we'd have other interests in common too; maybe we'd like the same foods or fashion designs.)*

Teacher Tip: If students are not sure about the Hebrew they need, it's fairly easy to find examples for many of these things online.

Building Activity: Paint a T-Shirt

If time and resources permit, have students create real tees that they can wear, based on their designs above, using white T-shirts, fabric makers, paints, stencils, etc.

Chapter 2 Lesson 2

A Study in Contrasts: Ancient and Modern, Diverse or Divided

Essential Question: How do traditional and modern factors shape the lives of Israelis today?

Learning Objectives: Students will be able to:

- Explain how Israel's ancient history influences modern Israeli life.
- Discuss why some Israelis might choose to live in more isolated communities, while others might seek multicultural experiences.
- Explore the choices Israeli students make in picking a school to attend.

Materials:

- Jerusalem Festival of Light video **(bhlink.me/israel2)**
- crayons or markers
- pictures of Israel from the internet, magazines, etc.
- glue
- poster board or kraft paper
- scissors
- three giant Post-it Notes, each with one of the questions from "Reflections: Talk about It" below

6Design a Modern/Ancient Show (10 minutes)

As students gather for class, play the video from the Jerusalem Festival of Light **(bhlink.me/israel2)**.

Explain to students:

> You're watching a video from the Jerusalem Festival of Light, in which an amazing light show is projected on the ancient walls of Jerusalem **(bhlink.me/israel2)**. What do you notice that's contemporary? What's ancient? *(ancient buildings and modern buildings, traditional symbols and high tech)* Imagine you had the chance to create your own light show, highlighting Israel's unique culture. What symbols would you include? Using crayons/markers or photos of Israel, draw or paste pictures onto the wall on page 31 of your books. Make each brick

reflect a different aspect of Israeli culture. (*Symbols may include: Hebrew letters, a menorah, falafel, modern Israeli art, a photo of an Israeli band, an Israeli celebrity like Gal Gadot.*)

Create Ads for Then and Now (10 minutes)

Say to students:

With a partner or in small groups, write two scripts for radio commercials. Each should advertise an Israeli store: one in ancient Israel and one today. What products do you think might have been available at the time of King David? What about today? What information would an ancient shopkeeper have wanted to tell customers? How about today's shop owner? *(Potential ideas for ancient shops: home-building materials, an apothecary for medicines, food for camels, scrolls and ink, musical instruments, wagons, animal skins. The ancient shopkeeper would likely focus on the practicality of the items, the fact that the next store might be many days travel away, the ways the products would aid in survival. Potential ideas for modern shops: food, clothing, technology, religious articles, artwork, pharmacy, movie theater. Today's shop owner would likely focus on convenience, lowest price, quality of materials offered, the desire to support the Israeli economy, etc.)*

If time permits, encourage each group to pick one script and perform it for the group. Or see the Building Activity immediately below.

Building Activity: Film a Commercial

In this activity, students turn their radio scripts ("Create Ads for Then and Now" above) into television commercials. Give students a few minutes to modify their scripts for filming, assign parts, and create props using classroom items or poster board, kraft paper, and other art supplies. Using tablets or smartphones, help students film their commercials.

Teacher Tip: Post the videos to a class website or send links to parents to view at home.

Diverse or Divided? Or Both? It's Complicated (10 minutes)

Invite volunteers to read pages 32 and the first paragraph of "Debate It!" on page 33.

Ask the class:

Should Oren go to a Jewish school or a multicultural school?

Have students pair up, or divide the group into two teams. Direct one side to argue why Oren should continue at a school that focuses on Jewish subjects; tell the other side to argue why Oren should switch to a multicultural school. After students have listed and discussed the main points they'd like to make, have the groups or teams debate the issue, taking turns presenting their arguments. *(Possible answers to the argument that Oren should choose to go to a Jewish-focused school include: It's important to understand Jewish culture and Zionist history as an Israeli citizen. Oren will have opportunities to meet Arabs later in life, through college and work experiences. He has many friends in his school, and it would be hard to start over somewhere new. Possible reasons why Oren might choose a multicultural school include: Israel as a whole benefits from opportunities for Arabs and Jews to get to know one another. Many believe this is one of the strongest paths forward to creating peace in the Middle East. Oren should open himself to new experiences.)*

Teacher Tip: Let students know that they don't necessarily have to agree with a side to argue that perspective. Remind students to be respectful of different opinions during the debate.

End this activity by asking students:

> Which type of school would you want to attend if you lived in Israel? Give students a minute to write their answer on the lines provided on page 33.

Encourage a few students to share their answers with the class.

Reflections: Talk about It! (15 minutes)

Hang the three giant Post-it Notes that you prepared earlier, each with one of the questions below, around the room. Divide the class into three groups; hand out pencils or pens. Have one group stand by each Post-it Note. Give each group a few minutes to write their answers to the question. Then have groups rotate to the left, with students adding answers to the new question or commenting on the answers of their classmates already on the Post-it Note. Rotate one more time so students will have had a chance to answer or comment on all three questions.

1. Think about your own community. What are some of the good things that come from diversity? What are some of the challenges? *(Some of the good things may include a variety of perspectives, beautiful music, delicious foods, exposure to different religions and cultures, etc. Some of the challenges may include discrimination, an inability to be on the same page, misunderstandings, etc.)*
2. What is the single most important thing you know about Israeli culture? What makes it so important to you? *(Potential answers may include: the many factors influencing Israel life because I value diversity, the ancient connections that Jews have to this land, the fact that Israelis share many of my interests because it helps me feel connected to Israel.)*
3. Imagine living in Israel for a year. What parts of Israeli culture would you most look forward to experiencing? *(delicious food, museums, the many opportunities for Jewish learning, spending time with Israelis, attending musical concerts and plays, learning Hebrew, visiting historical sites, etc.)*

As students add their answers and comments, circulate around the room and note especially interesting responses or questions that require further explanation. Discuss these with the class as a wrap-up to this chapter.

Teacher Tip: Save the Post-it Notes. It may be interesting to see how students' answers have changed by the time they've finished *Israel: It's Complicated.*

Additional Resources

The following activities and information can supplement the lessons or be used on their own to enrich learning about Israel as a mix of cultures.

Basic Law, 2018

Israel does not have a single constitution. The Basic Laws, passed by Knesset since 1950, make up the constitution of the State of Israel.

Basic Law: Israel-the Nation State of the Jewish People

Passed on July 19, 2018

Summary: The law determines, among other things, that the Land of Israel is the historical homeland of the Jewish people; the State of Israel is the nation state of the Jewish People, in which it realizes its natural, cultural, religious and historical right to self-determination; and that exercising the right to national self-determination in the State of Israel is unique to the Jewish People. The law also deals with the State's symbols and official language, the status of Jerusalem, the State's connection with the Jewish People and the Ingathering of Exiles.

Basic Principles	1. (a) The Land of Israel is the historical homeland of the Jewish people, in which the State of Israel was established.
	(b) The State of Israel is the nation state of the Jewish People, in which it realizes its natural, cultural, religious and historical right to self-determination.
	(c) The exercise of the right to national self-determination in the State of Israel is unique to the Jewish People.
State Symbols	2. (a) The name of the State is "Israel".
	(b) The State flag is white, with two light-blue stripes close to the edge, and a light-blue Star of David in its centre.
	(c) The State emblem is a seven-branched menorah with olive leaves on both sides, and the word "Israel" at its base.
	(d) The State anthem is "Hatikvah".
	(e) Details regarding the State symbols shall be determined by law.
State Capital	3. Jerusalem, complete and united, is the capital of Israel.

Basic Law, 2018 (continued)

Language	4. (a) Hebrew is the State language. (b) The Arabic language has a special status in the State; arrangements regarding the use of Arabic in state institutions or vis-à-vis them will be set by law. (c) Nothing in this article shall affect the status given to the Arabic language before this law came into force.
Ingathering of the Exiles	5. The State shall be open for Jewish immigration, and for the Ingathering of the Exiles.
The Connection with the Jewish People	6. (a) The State shall strive to ensure the safety of members of the Jewish People and of its citizens, who are in trouble and in captivity, due to their Jewishness or due to their citizenship. (b) The State shall act, in the Diaspora, to preserve the ties between the State and members of the Jewish People. (c) Nothing in this article shall affect the status given to the Arabic language before this law came into force.
Jewish Settlement	7. The State views the development of Jewish settlement as a national value, and shall act to encourage and promote its establishment and strengthening.
Official Calendar	8. The Hebrew calendar is an official calendar of the State, and the Gregorian calendar shall serve alongside it as an official calendar; the use of the Hebrew calendar and the Gregorian calendar shall be determined by law.
Independence Day and Memorial Days	9. (a) Independence Day is the official national holiday of the State. (b) Memorial Day for the Fallen in Israel's Wars, and the Holocaust Martyrs' and Heroes' Remembrance Day, are official memorial days of the state.
Days of Rest and Statutory Holidays	10. The Sabbath and the Jewish holidays are the established days of rest in the State; non-Jews have the right to observe the days of rest on their days of Sabbath and holidays; details regarding this matter shall be determined by law.
Entrenchment	11. This Basic law shall not be modified except by a Basic Law, passed by a majority of the members of the Knesset.

Source: The State of Israel, Knesset.gov

School Choices in Israel

Type of School	Languages taught	Religious subjects taught? (ie. Bible, religious law)	Regular subjects taught? (ie. math, science, history)	Who pays?
State secular public schools	Hebrew, Arabic, English. Depending on school, also other languages	Yes. But focus is on secular subjects.	Yes	The government—these schools are almost free, like public schools in U.S. Parents pay supplemental fees.
State Religious public schools	Hebrew, Arabic, English	Yes	Yes	The government—these schools are almost free, like public schools in the U.S. Parents pay supplemental fees.
Private Religious Schools	Depends on the school	Yes	Depends on the school. Ultra-orthodox Jewish schools will not teach these subjects but Arab-Christian private schools will.	Parents pay
Private Specialty School	Depends on the school	Depends on the specialty. Montessori school or American school will teach different subjects	Yes	Parents pay
TALI Schools (TALI is the Hebrew acronym for "Enriched Jewish Studies." TALI is a network of schools within the State secular schools. TALI adds Jewish studies to the learning day.	Hebrew, Arabic, English and maybe other languages, too	Yes	Yes	The government— these schools are almost free, like public schools in the U.S. Parents pay supplemental fees.

Compiled by Behrman House

New Meets Old as Kids Find Ancient Lamp

Times of Israel

1,400-year-old menorah lamp, rare coin found as kids dig trail for Israel's 70th

By Amanda Borschel-Dan, 16 April 2018

What can you give your country for its 70th anniversary? For thousands of school pupils and volunteers, the answer is the sweat of their brows as they worked to prepare a new public 70-kilometer (43-mile) walking path called the Sanhedrin Trail.

As a byproduct of their backbreaking work, they also stumbled upon a priceless 1,400-year-old intact oil lamp engraved with an eight-armed menorah, remains of important glass industry, and an extremely rare gold coin from Suleiman the Magnificent.

In the Galilee, where Jewish life was re-established 1,900 years ago after the bloody fall of the Second Temple, thousands of Israeli students and volunteers have created a "smart" trail connecting the different centers in which the Great Sanhedrin sat under the rule of the Roman Empire.

Tourists will be able to walk and learn about the archaeology, nature, and historical surroundings through high-tech milestones, which transmit information and activities directly to hikers' smartphones.

"There is no other a trail in Israel that utilizes such an application, and in this respect, we, the archaeologists, are making history," said Israel Antiquities Authority archaeologist Yair Amitzur.

According to Amitzur—the brains and much of the brawn behind the project — the pupils were "100 percent partners" in its development.

"It is the first place in Israel that is being founded as a site with GPS capabilities through the 'smart stones,'" Amitzur told *The Times of Israel*. (He acknowledged the name is a nod to the Hebrew translation of the Harry Potter books, as well as the traditional alchemist notion of a stone that can make gold.) Eventually, said Amitzur, the stones will also transmit augmented reality and 3-D visuals at each site.

"The Sanhedrin Trail is a huge project incorporating within it the values of nature, environment and history and is where the cultures of all of today's populations in the Galilee meet," said Amitzur.

He told *The Times of Israel* that the people and history of all three major monotheistic religions are represented along the trial, which makes use of newly renovated preexisting walking paths in as much as 80 percent of the route. In some places of mutual interest such as in Arbel or Kfar Kana, for example, the Sanhedrin Trail intersects with the popular 65-kilometer Jesus Trail. Another spot of international renown is the Horns of Hattin, the site of the infamous 1187 battle between the Crusaders and the Ayyubid sultan Salah ad-Din, Saladin.

Amitzur, who from personal experience says hiking the entirety of the trail takes about five days, hopes that in the future there will be organized camping sites along the route (so hikers don't need to sleep in the rough as he did).

Uncovering the past today, to prepare for tomorrow's future

While developing the trail, pupils participated in archaeological excavations at sites including Usha, the first seat of the Sanhedrin in the Galilee following the Bar Kochba revolt of 132-136 CE. Previous excavations of the small Galilee town site, as documented by the IAA's Hadashot website, have uncovered remains of a thriving community, including building foundations, a mosaic floor, rock-hewn tombs, wells, wine presses and an oil press.

"Based on the finds it was determined the site was continuously inhabited from the Roman period until the Ottoman period," according to a Hadashot report filed by Abdallah Massarwa following salvage excavations ahead of the construction of the Route 6 toll road.

During the recent excavations with the school pupils, more evidence of settlement was discovered, including an intact 1,400-year-old oil lamp engraved with an eight-staffed menorah, such as one would use during the holiday of Hanukkah. The menorah of the Temples, and the symbol of the State of Israel, only has seven staffs.

IAA archaeologist Dr. Einat Ambar-Armon, an expert on ancient clay lamps, said, "Unlike the modern day symbol of the state in which the Temple's menorah is depicted with seven branches and a single broad base, the menorah engraved on the ancient lamp has eight branches and a three-legged base. The discovery of a lamp decorated with a menorah, a symbol of the Jewish people, is without doubt exciting, especially at a site with such a unique heritage in part of the Sanhedrin Trail."

The menorah, said Amitzur in an IAA video about the project, "connects us to the continuity of the population here, which begins with the establishment of the Sanhedrin on the site, and continues with their descendants until the 7th century when we find this lamp as a distinctly Jewish symbol."

Additionally, said Amitzur, the team uncovered clear signs of the glass industry that is recorded in ancient Jewish sources as having been located in the vicinity of Usha.

This glass manufacturing was one of the most important centers of glass manufacturing during the Roman Empire, he said. Its quality was considered very fine—the discovered blocks are still crystal clear—and would have been exported throughout the empire.

After Usha, the Sanhedrin moved on to Shefar`am in 140 CE, then to Bet She'arim and Zippori in 163 CE, until it was finally established in Tiberias in 193 CE.

There's gold in them thar hills

While helping to connect the dots along the route, high school student Ilai Yonah, a student at Ha-Moshava High School in Zikhron Ya`akov, uncovered a gold coin bearing an inscription from the period of sultan Suleiman the Magnificent, ruler of the Ottoman Empire and builder of Jerusalem's city walls, who died in 1566. Only two others exist in the State Treasury.

"As I was walking I was looking at the ground," said Yonah in the IAA video. "I saw something gold. I saw it was some kind of coin with Arabic writing. I brought it to one of the archaeologists. I thought it was something ancient, but not to this extent." Another student who spotted the coin along with Yonah laughed and said, "We thought they [the archaeologists] were trying to fool us." "That they put it there on purpose," added a stunned Yonah, holding the coin.

New Meets Old as Kids Find Ancient Lamp (continued)

According to Amitzur, the coin is but one artifact depicting the "variety of periods, cultures and stories" found along the trail.

"This is a flagship project that connects the future generation preparing the trail to its heritage and to the Jewish people's great and inspiring leaders. The trail is a groundbreaking endeavor utilizing state of the art technologies in order to connect with our roots" said Israel Hasson, director of the Israel Antiquities Authority, in a press release.

The IAA received help to bring the educational-tourism project to fruition from the Ministry of Jerusalem and Heritage—Landmarks Project, Finance Ministry, National Religious Education Administration (Hemed) and the Shelah Department of the Education Ministry, municipalities, local and regional councils, Nature and Parks Authority, Jewish National Fund and others.

For the students, they now have a unique connection to the land they worked. The "gift" of this new impressive path to their country was given right back to them.

"We learn a lot in class," said Tal Dothan from Neve Dekalim Ulpana in Nitzan. "But in practice, when does it sink in? When you walk the trail, when you feel it. When you dig with a pickax and blaze a trail in the country, you appreciate the country much more."

Chapter 3

It's Religious

In This Chapter

Introduction

Enduring Understanding:

The Jewish people have an enduring religious and historical bond to the Land of Israel; the land has long been significant to Christians, Muslims, and others as well.

Chapter Overview:

This chapter explores the Jewish connection to the land of Israel from biblical times, to the days of the Temple, to the modern day. It also examines the relationships of other religions to Israel and explores some of the compromises and challenges that arise in order to share access to holy sites.

Words to Know:

Al-Aqsa Mosque: Muslim place of worship, built on the Temple Mount

Church of the Holy Sepulchre: stands on the site on which Christians believe Jesus's crucifixion took place

Dome of the Rock: the gold-topped shrine in Jerusalem that Islam teaches is the place from which the Muslim prophet Muhammad ascended to heaven

Kotel: the Western Wall of the ancient Second Temple; Judaism's holiest site

Lech L'cha/L'chi lach (masculine/feminine forms): "go for yourself" in Hebrew

Via Dolorosa: Christianity teaches that Jesus walked on this path on the way to his crucifixion

Chapter 3 Lesson 1
The Jewish Bond to Israel

Essential Question: How have Jews remained connected to the land of Israel for thousands of years?

Learning Objectives: Students will be able to:

- Identify the first Jews to come to the land of Israel.
- Understand the role the Temple played in Jewish and Israeli history, and the role the Kotel plays in modern life.
- Discuss how Jewish bonds to the Land of Israel have been expressed through art and music.

Materials Needed:

- Costumes for Abraham and Sarah skit (optional)
- "L'chi Lach" by Debbie Friedman (bhlink.me/israel3)
- "My Heart Is in the East" by Dan Nichols (bhlink.me/israel3)
- "Hope" by the Fountainheads (bhlink.me/israel3)
- Crayons and/or markers

Activities

What Do You See? (5 minutes)

Write the following questions on the board. As students arrive, ask them to find a partner, look at the pictures on pages 34 and 35 of their books, and discuss the questions:

- What do the images have in common? How are they different? *(Images all portray people engaged in some form of prayer. The people praying are from a variety of religions, using different approaches to prayer.)*
- What do you see in the photos that tells you something religious is happening? *(Some people are holding prayer books, others wear religious garb, the people appear to be at holy sites, etc.)*

The Jewish Connection (10 minutes)

Invite a volunteer to read the Torah text found on page 34 of the student book. Then, play Debbie Friedman's song "L'chi Lach" for your students **(bhlink.me/israel3)**. Have them work with partners to discuss questions 1 and 2 at the top of page 34:

- Compare Debbie Friedman's song with the Torah text found on page 34. How are they similar? Different? *(Since Friedman's song is based on this text, they carry similar messages. Friedman's song highlights the fact that Abraham and Sarah specifically do not know the land. Friedman's song adds that people will praise Sarah's name in addition to Abraham's.)*

- Imagine that you received the same message. How would you feel about moving to a new land, especially one that you knew almost nothing about? *(Students might imagine feeling excited about going to a new place, nervous about facing the unknown, or sad to leave the people and places they love behind.)*

When students have answered these questions, ask them as a class:

- How is it different to move to a new land today? How does that shape your perception of Abraham and Sarah? *(With technology and modern transportation, it is fairly easy to stay in touch with loved ones and to visit. In Abraham and Sarah's time, they left knowing they probably would never see or speak to their loved ones again. Some students may feel this increases their appreciation for Abraham and Sarah's courage and dedication; other students may feel sad for them.)*

- How would you feel if you were told that you and your children would become "a great nation" and that you would "be a blessing?" What does that mean to you? Would you be excited? Overwhelmed? Humbled? *(When God promised Abraham and Sarah that they would become "a great nation," God meant that they would become the parents of the Jewish people; being a blessing to others can mean bringing goodness into the lives of other people. Students might be honored by these ideas or intimidated by them.)*

Lech L'cha Script (10 minutes)

In groups of three or four, ask students to create a skit in which Abraham and Sarah discuss whether to accept God's commandment to go to a new land. Students should consider:

What concerns might Abraham and Sarah have? What might Abraham and Sarah be excited about? Nervous about?

Students can write their scripts on page 35 of their books or on a separate sheet of paper. Invite students to share their scripts with the class. If time allows, students can act out their skits. *(Skits might highlight uncertainty about whether or how to believe in God. Abraham and Sarah might be frightened about the dangers of the journey to a new land and what they might find when they get there. They might be sad to leave friends and family behind. They might struggle to explain their reasoning, especially since they were the first to believe in one God.)*

Text Study: Connections to Israel (15 minutes)

Together or in small groups, read the poem "My Heart Is in the East," by Yehudah Halevi, found on page 37 of *Israel...It's Complicated.*

Explain to students that Yehudah Halevi, a Jewish philosopher, poet, and physician, was born in Spain. Toward the end of his life he traveled to Egypt and from there planned to go to Israel. It is unclear whether he made it to Israel before his death.

Ask:

> What does Halevi mean when he says his "heart is in the east"? *(He is expressing his longing for Israel: though he lives in Spain—the west—his heart is in the east—Israel.)* What does he mean when he writes that "Zion lieth beneath the fetter of Edom, and I in Arab chains"? *(Edom refers to Christianity. At the time Halevi was writing his poem, Israel was under Christian control, while Spain was under Muslim control.)*

Explain that modern Jewish musicians continue to share the sentiments expressed by Yehudah Halevei centuries ago. Then, play the songs "My Heart Is in the East" by Dan Nichols and "Hope" by the Fountainheads, which can be found at **bhlink.me/israel3**.

Ask students:

> What do the modern songs have in common with Yehudah Halevi's ancient poem? What themes do they share? *(Both the poem and the songs share a yearning to be in Eretz Yisrael. Yehudah Halevi may never have expected to reach Israel. The songs are more optimistic, expressing hopes and dreams for a land that is real and a part of their lives.)*

Say:

> In the sheet music at the bottom of page 37 of your books, write the emotions each artist expresses. In the last row, describe how listening to their words made you feel. *(Students might express sympathy for Yehuda Halevi when reading his poem. When listening to Dan Nichols, they might feel optimistic, hopeful, or cheerful; they might imagine visiting Israel themselves, or envision the connection to Israel as a love story between Israel and the Jewish people. When listening to the Fountainheads, students might feel energized, excited, connected to Israel as our homeland; they might even feel like dancing!)*

Continue:

> Music is a great way to feel connected to Israel. What other Jewish traditions today help us feel connected to Israel? *(We pray facing toward Jerusalem; our prayers may include a wish to return to Jerusalem/Zion; we break a glass at Jewish weddings to remind us of the destruction of the Temple; we end our Passover s'darim with the wish, "Next year in Jerusalem.")*

Building Activity: Make Some Music

Say to the class:

> With a partner, agree on a song you both like. Write new lyrics to that music expressing the Jewish people's passion for Israel or your own connection to the Jewish homeland. (If you don't want to write a song, write a poem instead.)

Give students a chance to perform their songs or poems for the group. Invite another class to join the audience. Film the performances and share them with parents.

Letters in the Kotel (5 minutes)

Invite volunteers to read aloud page 36, beginning with "Temple Times" and ending with the first paragraph of "The Kotel."

Hand out pencils/pens and paper to students and say:

> Imagine you are placing a note in the Kotel. What would you wish or pray for in your note? Write your note on the sheet of paper in front of you.

If time permits, encourage students to share their notes with the class or post them on a classroom wall or bulletin board, perhaps with background decoration that looks like a stone wall.

Building Activity: Insert a Note in the Kotel

As a class, compose a note to be inserted in the Kotel. Visit **bhlink.me/israel3** to learn how to send your class's message to the actual Kotel.

Building Activity: The Kotel Responds

Say to students:

> Imagine that the Kotel could write a note back to you. What do you think it would want to say to you, a person living in the twenty-first century? What wisdom might the Kotel be able to share with you from the many centuries it has spent observing people? How does the Kotel feel living in the modern Jewish country of Israel? Write its note to you on the back of the note you wrote.

Chapter 3 Lesson 2

Sharing Sacred Space

Essential Question: If Israel is sacred to so many religions, how can we work together to share spaces?

Learning Objectives: Students will be able to:

- Articulate the connections between other religious groups and the land of Israel.
- Understand that members of different religions have their own unique perspectives on Israel.
- Discuss how sharing spaces can create challenges.

Materials Needed:

- Glue sticks or rolls of tape (at least one per group)
- Scissors (at least one pair per group)
- Markers (at least two per group)
- Printed photos from the Internet, magazines, etc., of places that might be important to students for the "Can You Share Your Space?" activity (examples include a bedroom, a vacation spot, a soccer field, a local park; students can also be encouraged in advance to bring to class a photo of a favorite place).

Activities

Getting Started (5 minutes)

Invite volunteers to read aloud the text and captions about Muslim, Christian, Druze, and Baha'i connections to Israel on page 38 of *Israel... It's Complicated.*

Ask students:

> What are some of the benefits to Israel of being a holy site to so many religions? What might be some of the challenges? *(Benefits: You learn about many different religions; you learn about unfamiliar traditions; you learn to be respectful of other people's beliefs. Challenges: The teachings of one religion may seem to conflict with the teachings of another; sites that are holy to one faith may also be holy to another faith, making it difficult to share.)*

Building Activity: Sacred Sites of Israel

Divide students into small groups. Have each group research one of the holy sites mentioned in their books: Dome of the Rock, Al-Aqsa Mosque, Via Dolorosa, Church of the Holy Sepulchre, Tomb of Nabi Shu'ayb, Baha'i Gardens, Tomb of the Báb. Then, invite them to share more about these places with the class through an interview or in a video made on their phones or tablets.

What Do You See? (10 minutes)

Ask students to quickly look at the image at the top of page 39 of their books and, on the lines provided, write down what they see. *(Students may see either a tree or two people facing each other.)*

Then, ask them to look at the picture again and write what they see. On second glance, do they see it differently?

Divide students into pairs and have them discuss the following questions with a partner:

- How did your thinking about the picture change after you realized that there was more than one way to see it? *(It forced me to concentrate on the picture. It was cool to see two different possibilities in the image. It was a little confusing to realize that my friends had seen something totally different than I had.)*
- People from many faiths—Jews, Christians, Muslims, and others—come to visit Jerusalem. In what ways do you think they might see Jerusalem similarly? Differently? *(Many people see Jerusalem as a holy site and feel a connection to the historical aspects of the city. They might appreciate Jerusalem's beauty and the many interesting things it has to offer. Some may feel hurt or frustrated due to the conflicts that have occurred here throughout the years. Some may connect more to specific quarters—Jewish, Christian, Muslim, Armenian—depending on their own background.)*
- In what ways did learning that Jerusalem means different things to people of different faiths change your own understanding of Jerusalem? *(It made Jerusalem more real to me. It was helpful to see the complexity involved and interesting to learn the perspectives of others. It made me sad that a city I love could be a place that causes hurt in others.)*

Can You Share Your Space? (20 minutes)

Say to the class:

> *Sacred sites in Israel are often considered holy by more than one religion, and compromises are often made when groups share access to holy sites.*

Invite volunteers to read "Sharing the Temple Mount," Sharing the Church of the Holy Sepulchre," and "Does Sharing Work?" on page 40 of their books.

Break the class up into groups of three or four, then say:

> On separate pieces of paper, each of you make your own collage about a place that is important to you. BUT, as a group, you only get one glue stick or roll of tape, one pair of scissors, and just two markers. After five minutes, you can add more supplies to your table. *(If students have difficulty thinking of a place, suggest their bedroom, grandparents' house, a place they like to go on vacation, etc.)*

After students have had time to complete their collages, have them discuss the following:

- How did it feel to have to share the supplies for your project? *(It was okay at first, then it got a little frustrating. It meant I had to be really organized and plan for my time with the supplies. It turned us into a team, to ensure we could help each other complete the project.)*
- What might have happened if one of you had refused to share one of the supplies? *(I would have gotten really upset. It might have meant we weren't able to finish our assignment. We would have had to ask for help from the teacher. We might have had to ask another group to borrow a specific supply.)*
- What if, instead of simple art supplies, the things you were asked to share were important to you? How would it have felt to share your most prized possession? *(It might depend on who I was sharing with; it's easier to share with someone I care about than a stranger. It would be frustrating. I would be afraid that my possession might be damaged. I might resent having to share.)*

Building Activity: Sharing in Real Life

In pairs, encourage students to recount a real situation in which they had to share something—say with a sibling or a camp bunkmate. How did that experience play out? Was there something that made it work? Was there an obstacle to success? What might their personal experience teach them about what life is like in Israel? If time permits, allow students to share their examples with the class or act them out in a short skit.

Reflection: Talk about It! (10 minutes)

With a partner, have students answer the following questions:

- Describe an emotional connection that you have to a place. It could be a building, like your home or school, or something smaller like the corner of your room. It could be the place you made a collage about earlier. *(Students might say they connect to a place because of the people who share it with them. A specific place might help them feel safe or might evoke a happy memory. Students might also say that a place makes them feel sad because it reminds them of someone that they lost.)*
- If you traveled to Israel, which of the holy sites would you like to visit? Would you want to visit one that is sacred to a religion other than your own? *(Students might be interested in visiting the Kotel, the Baha'i Gardens, the Church of the Holy Sepulchre, etc.)*
- How do you think you might feel on your visit? How might those feelings be similar to or different from your feelings when you visit the spot you described in your answer to the first question? *(Students might be excited about visiting Israel or nervous about being somewhere different. It might feel different than the place they mentioned in question 1 because they don't have the same level of personal connection. They might be curious about the things around them and look forward to learning more. They might feel connected to the history and heritage of the land. It might feel like being at home, since they have learned so much about Israel.)*

Additional Resources

The following activities and information can supplement the lessons or be used on their own to enrich learning about religious connections to Israel.

The Promised Land: A *Chevruta* Activity

By Marc Rosenstein and Tova Sacher

Introduction

The question of what connects the Jewish people to the Land of Israel is one of both history and belief. The Bible recounts the Patriarchs' arrival and residence in the land of Canaan. They trekked through the land and farmed it. Our traditions speak of a divine promise bestowing the land to their descendants. The fledgling nation of Israel leaves Egypt and embarks on a journey to the Promised Land. Joshua conquers the land because of his belief in such a promise, and the tribes of Israel settle it. The prophets speak of a messianic return to the land as a lasting fulfillment of God's oath, and traditional Jewish prayers repeatedly recall it. These biblical references lie at the core of our collective memory connecting us to the land. It was these traditions that helped ignite modern Zionism,

How does the biblical promise affect our emotional and physical connection to the land? In this lesson we hope to familiarize students with both biblical and historical connections between the Land of Israel and the Jewish people that exist in our tradition and collective memory.

The Activity (25–30 minutes)

1. Divide the class into small groups of two or three students. Distribute copies of the text for the *chevruta* study, the questions, and the text study review (see following pages). Assign one of the five texts to each group.
2. Give each group about 15 minutes to study their assigned text and to respond to the questions about the Land of Israel as promised to the Jewish people by God. Tell the students to be sure to give specific text examples in their statement and to be prepared to present their answers to the questions to the class. (The Teacher Reference Sheet includes additional background information.)
3. After about fifteen minutes, bring the class back together. Have each group present their findings to the rest of the class.
4. Have students complete the Text Study Review while the other groups are presenting their texts. Once each group has presented its text, review this page as a class. Answers are provided on the answer key *(see page 62)*.

—From *CHAI Israel Strand Curriculum Core*, URJ Press

The Promised Land: Texts for *Chevruta* Study

1 Genesis 12:1–7: God Appears to Abram for the First Time

The Eternal One said to Abram, "Go forth from your land, your birthplace, your father's house, to the land that I will show you. I will make of you a great nation, and I will bless you, I will make your name great, and it shall be a blessing. I will bless those who bless you, and I will pronounce doom on those who curse you; through you all the families of the earth shall be blessed." So Abram went forth as the Eternal had told him, and Lot went with him. Abram was seventyfive (75 years old when he left Haran. Abram took his wife Sarai, his brother's son Lot, all the possessions they had amassed, and the people they had acquired in Haran. They set forth for the land of Canaan, and they arrived in the land of Canaan. Abram then traversed the land as far as the sacred site of Shechem, as far as the Oak of Moreh. (At that time the Canaanites were present in the land.).

The Eternal now appeared to Abram and said, "I am giving this land to your descendants." Abram then built an altar there to the Eternal who had appeared to him.

2 Genesis 28:10–22: Jacob's Dream

And Jacob left Beersheba and set out for Haran. Coming upon a [certain] place, he passed the night there, for the sun was setting; taking one of the stones of the place, he made it his head-rest as he lay down in that place. He dreamed, and lo—a ladder was set on the ground, with its top reaching to heaven, and lo—angels of God going up and coming down on it. And lo-the Eternal stood up above it, and said, "I, the Eternal, am the God of your father Abraham and God of Isaac: the land on which you are lying I will give to you and to your descendants. And your descendants shall be like the dust of the earth, and you shall spread out to the west and the east and the north and the south. Through you and your descendants all the families of the earth shall find blessing. And here I am, with you: I will watch over you wherever you go, and I will bring you back to this soil. I will not let go of you as long as I have yet to do what I have promised you."

Waking from his sleep, Jacob said, "Truly, the Eternal is in this place, and I did not know it!" He was awestruck, and said, "How awe-inspiring is this place! This is none other than the house of God, and this is the gate of heaven!"

Rising early that morning, Jacob took the stone that he had put under his head and set it up as a monument. He then poured oil on its top. He named that place Beth EL (But originally the town's name was Luz.) Jacob then made this vow: "If God is with me and watches over me on this path that I am taking and gives me bread to eat and clothes to wear, and if I return safely to my father's house, then will the Eternal be my God; and this stone that I have set up as a monument shall be a house of God. And [of] all that You give me, I will dedicate a tenth to You."

3 Exodus 3:1–12, 16–18: The Burning Bush

Now Moses, tending the flock of his father-in-law Jethro, the priest of Midian, drove the flock into the wilderness, and came to Horeb, the mountain of God. An angel of the Eternal appeared to him in a blazing fire out of a bush. He gazed, and there was a bush all aflame, yet the bush was not consumed. Moses said, "I must turn aside to look at this marvelous sight; why doesn't the bush burn up?" When the Eternal saw that he had turned aside to look, God called to him out of the bush: "Moses! Moses!" He answered, "Here I am." And [God] said, "Do not come closer! Remove your sandals from your feet, for the place on which you stand is holy ground!" and continued, "I am the God of your ancestors-the God of Abraham, the God of Isaac, and the God of Jacob." And Moses hid his face, for he was afraid to look at God.

And the Eternal continued, "I have marked well the plight of My people in Egypt and have heeded their outcry because of their taskmasters; yes, I am mindful of their sufferings. I have come down to rescue them from the Egyptians and to bring them out of that land to a good and spacious land, a land flowing with milk and honey, the region of the Canaanites, the Hittites, the Amorites, the Perizzites, the Hivites, and the Jebusites. Now the cry of the Israelites has reached Me; moreover, I have seen how the Egyptians oppress them. Come, therefore, I will send you to Pharaoh, and you shall free My people, the Israelites, from Egypt."

But Moses said to God, "Who am I that I should go to Pharaoh and free the Israelites from Egypt?" And [God] said, "I will be with you; that shall be your sign that it was I who sent you. And when you have freed the people from Egypt, you shall worship God at this mountain...

Go and assemble the elders of Israel and say to them: the Eternal, the God of your ancestors-the God of Abraham, Isaac, and Jacob-has appeared to me and said, 'I have taken note of you and of what is being done to you in Egypt, and I have declared: I will take you out of the misery of Egypt to the land of the Canaanites, the Hittites, the Amorites, the Perizzites, the Hivites, and the Jebusites, to a land flowing with milk and honey.' They will listen to you; then you shall go with the elders of Israel to the king of Egypt and you shall say to him, 'The Eternal, the God of the Hebrews, became manifest to us. Now therefore, let us go a distance of three days into the wilderness to sacrifice to the Eternal our God.'"

4 Joshua 1:1–7

After the death of Moses, the servant of the Eternal, the Eternal said to Joshua son of Nun, Moses' assistant, "My servant Moses is dead; come now, come across this [river] Jordan, you and all this people, and go into the land that I am giving to the people of Israel. As I promised Moses, I am giving you every foot of ground you step on. Your borders [shall reach] from the desert [in the south] and the Lebanon [in the north] to the great River, the river Euphrates [in the east]-[that is] all the land of the Hittites-to the Great Sea in the west. As long as you live, no one shall be able to stand against you. I will be with you as I was with Moses. I will never fail you or leave you.

"Be strong and of good courage, for you must bring this people into possession of the land that I swore to their ancestors to give to them. Only be strong and of good courage in observing faithfully all the Torah that Moses My servant commanded you; do not turn away from it to the right or to the left: then you shall do well wherever you go.

5 Ezekiel 36:8–12, 22, 24, 27–28

Mountains of Israel bloom forth your trees and give your fruits to My people Israel, for they are at hand to come... You shall be tilled and planted. And I will multiply men upon you, all of the House of Israel and the cities shall be inhabited and the destroyed places built up. I will multiply upon you man and animals and they shall be fruitful. I will cause you to be inhabited as before and be better than your beginnings. And you will know that I am the Eternal. And I will bring back My people, Israel, and you will be for them an inheritance... So say to the House of Israel: ... I will gather you from all the lands, and I will bring you to your land ... and I will put My spirit in your midst and you will walk in My ways and keep My commandments. You will dwell in the land that I gave to your fore fathers, and you will be My people and I will be your God.

The Promised Land: Questions

According to the text, why is God promising the land at this point? What is the situation? Why is the promise necessary?

Was there anything done to deserve this promise?

Are there any conditions?

Are there other promises made in this text?

—From *CHAI Israel Strand Curriculum Core*, URJ Press

The Promised Land: Text Study Review

1 Genesis 12:1–7

God told Abraham to ______________________________.

After Abraham arrived in ____________ God promised ______________________________

______________________________.

2 Genesis 28:10–22

Jacob dreamed about ______________________________.

God spoke to Jacob and promised:

1 ______________________________

2 ______________________________

When Jacob woke up, he ______________________________.

3 Exodus 3:1–12, 16–18

Moses saw a ______________________________

God spoke to Moses and said ______________________________

______________________________.

God told Moses to gather the elders and tell them ______________________________

______________________________.

4 Joshua 1:1–7

God spoke to Joshua and promised:

1 ______________________________

2 ______________________________

God told Joshua he must:

1 ______________________________

2 ______________________________

3 Ezekiel 36:8–12, 22, 24, 27–28

God promises Ezekiel that:

1 The mountains shall bloom ____________________ and give ______________

______________________________.

2 The people of Israel will ______________________________
and they will ______________________________.

3 The land will be ______________________________.

The Promised Land: Answer Key to Text Study Review

1 **Genesis 12:1–7**

God told Abraham to leave his home and land and go to where God tells him. After Abraham arrived in the land/Canaan God promised to give this land to his children/descendants.

2 **Genesis 28:10–22**

Jacob dreamed about a ladder reaching from the earth to the sky with angels on it.

God spoke to Jacob and promised:

- Give him/his children the land he is lying on.
- Make his children many/spread them throughout the land.

When Jacob woke up he made a monument to God/promised to give God one-tenth of everything if God kept God's promise.

3 **Exodus 3:1–12, 16–18**

Moses saw a burning bush.

God spoke to Moses and said that God had seen the suffering of God's people and was going to bring them out of Egypt.

God told Moses to gather the elders and tell them God was taking them out of Egypt and bringing them to the land flowing with milk and honey.

4 **Joshua 1:1–7**

God spoke to Joshua and promised:

- God would give them every part of the land they walk on.
- God would be with and help them. No one would stop them.

God told Joshua he must:

- Be strong and brave.
- Observe God's laws and commandments.

5 **Ezekiel 36:8–12, 22, 24, 27–28**

God promises Ezekiel that:

- The mountains shall bloom flowers and give fruit.
- The people of Israel will return to live in the land and they will keep God's laws.
- The land will be built up/full of people.

—From *CHAI Israel Strand Curriculum Core*, URJ Press

The Promised Land: Teacher Reference Sheet

	Genesis 12	Genesis 28	Exodus 3	Joshua 1	Ezekiel 36
Why is God promising the land at this point?	Abraham obeyed God and left his home–needs to know where he belongs. He arrives in a land full of other people. Why is he here?	Jacob has to run away and leave. What about the future? Will he come back?	God tells Moses to take the people out of Egypt—they need to know where they are going.	Joshua is going to lead the people in a war for the land—needs to know that God is with him.	The people are in exile; they need to know if they will ever come back to the land. Is it still theirs?
Was there anything done to deserve this promise?	He listened to God—left his home and family.	Not mentioned—maybe in Abraham and Isaac's merit.	Not mentioned.	Not mentioned.	Not mentioned.
Are there any conditions?	Not mentioned.	Not mentioned—maybe act like Abraham; listen to God.	Not mentioned.	Keep God's commandments.	God says the people will keep God's commandments.
Reasons?	Not mentioned—perhaps because Abraham believed in God and listened to God and left his home to come to Canaan.	Not mentioned - maybe to keep God's promise to Abraham and Isaac.	God sees the people's suffering and remembers God's promise to their forefathers.	To keep God's promise to the forefathers and the children of Israel.	Dwell in the land God gave to their forefathers, to be God's people, and God will be their God.
Are there other promises made in this text?	Children—Abraham has no children; God promises the land to his descendants.	Many descendants; watch over him; bring him back.	To save them, take them out of Egypt. The land is good.	God will be with you; success; borders.	The land will bloom; gather them from all over.
What does one have to do?	Not mentioned—maybe keep believing and listening to God.	Not mentioned.	Not mentioned—God says they will believe Moses.	Be strong and brave; lead; keep God's laws.	Not mentioned—maybe keep God's faith and laws.
Reactions?	Builds an altar—Thanksgiving.	Jacob makes a deal—if God keeps God's promise, he will give God a tenth.	Moses is hesitant.	Not mentioned—afterwards he prepares for war.	Not mentioned.

—From *CHAI Israel Strand Curriculum Core*, URJ Press

Christian Holy Site in Jerusalem Has Muslim Gatekeeper

Muslims (literally) Hold Key to Jerusalem's Church of the Holy Sepulcher

By Judith Sudilovsky, *Catholic News Service*
2.27.2018

JERUSALEM -- Jerusalem's most famous Christian church, shared by three denominations, is unlocked each morning by a Muslim.

Since the seventh century, the family of Wajeeh Nuseibeh, 69, has handed down the responsibility of opening the door of the Church of the Holy Sepulcher.

"If the key would be in the hands of the Greek Orthodox, then that would signify they are the owners of the church. If it is the hands of the Catholics, then it would be a Catholic Church, the same with the Armenians (Orthodox)" Nuseibeh said in a 1999 interview. "So Muslims are neutral people to open and close the door."

Nuseibeh was the one to officially close the doors of the church Feb. 25 as the heads of churches announced its indefinite closure to protest for Israeli measures they described as a "systematic campaign ... against the churches and the Christian community in the Holy Land." He said he felt very saddened by the turn of the events.

"I am very sad pilgrims are coming from distances to come here ... they come to visit the church and are not able to see it because of a mistake made by the mayor" of Jerusalem to charge property taxes on church-owned property, he said. "Only if pilgrims stop coming will he stop with the issues of taxes. There will be more problems until this is solved with the municipality. I get my orders from the Greek Orthodox, the Armenian and the Catholic. Not from the government."

Since the time of the Turkish rule in Jerusalem, another Muslim family, the Joudehs, has been responsible for holding the key. The Joudeh and Nuseibeh families employ another Muslim man to open the doors early most mornings.

Nuseibeh arrives to take his post at 9 a.m. and spends most of his day near the entrance of the church.

As a child, Nuseibeh used to visit the church with his father, Jacob. Wajeeh Nuseibeh took over his father's position when he died in 1986. His father had held the position since 1967, when he replaced his cousin.

In a place like the Church of the Holy Sepulcher, where the 1885 Status Quo agreement is guarded by all the Christian groups in the church, this responsibility is no small matter, and the centuries-old traditions are taken very seriously.

"If he didn't open the door, it would stay shut," the late Dominican Father Jerome Murphy-O'Connor, a professor at L'Ecole Biblique said in 1999. "It is crucial to the maintenance of the whole Status Quo. If things were to change, then all the elements of the agreement would be up for grabs, and I don't think any of the churches would be interested in that."

During most of the year, Nuseibeh's job consists of keeping track of when and how to open the door, depending on which group is having a religious procession and what time it is. Every afternoon at 4 p.m., he shuts the door halfway to signal the beginning of the Franciscan procession and to keep people from entering or leaving to prevent disruption of the event.

"My father showed me everything, what to do and what is the right way to do it. He wrote down notes and explained it to me," said Nuseibeh.

The February protest closure was only the second time the doors have been shut off schedule, said Nuseibeh. Twenty years ago, the church was closed because of a disturbance caused by a visitor to the church, he said.

Every inch of the church is so carefully watched over by the different denominations that even the ladder used to reach the window in front of the door's padlock is under contention. Sometimes it is symbolically in the possession of the Armenian Orthodox, or the Greek Orthodox or the Catholics. It is Nuseibeh's responsibility to pound the heavy door knocker on the ancient doors, signifying the figurative changing of ownership of the ladder.

The busiest time of the year for Nuseibeh is the week before Easter (Holy Week). During that week, Nuseibeh gets the key from the Joudeh family, and opens the door at 4 a.m.

Traditionally on a day when all three denominations have a holy day, representatives of the Greek, Armenian and Catholic churches unbolt the door from inside, then pass the ladder outside the trap-door window, where it is received and placed upon the door.

Nuseibeh then climbs the ladder, a representative of the Joudeh family gives him the key, and he opens the lock. A bell inside is rung to announce the opening, and the three representatives open the inside lock and, at the signal, pull the handle together. Finally, they all go outside to take the ladder inside.

On Holy Thursday, the key is temporarily given to the vicar of the Franciscan Custody of the Holy Land. That afternoon he is the one who hands the key to Nuseibeh to open the door, then it is once again returned to the Joudeh family.

On Good Friday, said Nuseibeh, the key is given to the Greek Orthodox in a similar fashion. The same ritual is followed for the Holy Fire ceremony for the Armenian Orthodox. Nuseibeh also plays a role in this traditional ceremony and is a witness to the sealing of the tomb of Jesus.

Discussions about opening a new emergency door to the church have never been completed, although the three denominations have agreed on a location.

"If there were to be a second door, who would be in charge of the key?" asked Father Murphy-O'Connor almost two decades ago. "If there is an emergency, who would have the key? It's very complex when you start thinking of the details."

The question remains unanswered.

Security at the Temple Mount, a Shared Sacred Space

Israel Agrees to Remove Metal Detectors at Temple Mount

JULY 24, 2017

(JTA) — Israel will remove metal detectors from entrances to the Temple Mount after days of rioting by Palestinians furious at the installation of the devices in the wake of a deadly terrorist attack.

"The Security Cabinet accepted the recommendation of all of the security bodies to incorporate security measures based on advanced technologies ('smart checks') and other measures instead of metal detectors in order to ensure the security of visitors and worshippers in the Old City and on the Temple Mount," said a government statement released late Monday night.

The statement said Israel will pay up to 100 million shekels (about $30 million) over the next six months to install the new devices, which Haaretz reported include technologically advanced security cameras.

The area around the Temple Mount, the holiest site in Judaism and also the location of the Haram A-Sharif, the third holiest site in Islam, has been riven with tensions since July 14, when three Arab-Israelis shot and killed two Israeli police officers there before they were shot to death.

Israeli authorities installed the metal detectors at the site in the wake of the attack. Muslims since then have refused to enter the Temple Mount, instead praying outside of its gates, leading to clashes and the deaths of at least five Palestinians in recent days.

The announcement came after days of intensive consultations among Prime Minister Benjamin Netanyahu, Jordanian King Abdullah and the Trump administration, including President Donald Trump's special envoy to the region, Jason Greenblatt, who flew in Sunday to help calm the tensions.

Chapter 4 It's a Jewish Democracy

Words to Know:

Knesset: Israel's legislative (law-making) branch of government; seats are based on votes for a political party rather than for an individual

Women of the Wall (WOW): a group of women who meet monthly to pray at the Kotel. Their prayer services are often met with protests by ultra-Orthodox Jews.

Introduction

Enduring Understanding:

Israel's political system reflects ideals and values based on both democracy and Judaism.

Chapter Overview:

This chapter explores the Jewish and democratic values that shape the State of Israel. Students will gain a deeper understanding of how the Knesset works, including debating controversial issues and forming coalitions to pass laws.

Chapter 4 Lesson 1

A Democratic State

Essential Question: How do democratic values shape the State of Israel?

Learning Objectives: Students will be able to:

- Articulate freedoms that citizens of a democracy enjoy.
- Explain that Israelis vote for political parties rather than specific candidates.
- Demonstrate how disagreement and collaboration shape the work of the Knesset.

Materials:

- poster board (one per student)
- markers
- paints and paint brushes
- pictures of Israel
- glue
- scissors
- two signs: "Agree" and "Disagree"
- Comparison of Governments chart (found on page 75 of this guide)

Activities

Getting Started (10 minutes)

Before students enter the classroom, make two lists on the board:

Base	Fillings and Toppings
milk chocolate	sprinkles
dark chocolate	chopped nuts
white chocolate	chocolate chips
	peanut butter chips
	raisins
	peppermint cream
	toffee bits
	crisped rice
	your favorite candy

After students arrive, have students work with a partner to invent a new candy bar. Each bar can have up to three fillings or toppings. They can use the list on the board or come up with their own ingredients. Ask them:

> When you disagree about what fillings or toppings to use, how can you compromise to create a candy bar you'd both like to eat?

Invite students to share their answers with the class. Finish by explaining that this lesson is about Israel's government. In order to pass laws in the Knesset, Israel's legislative body, political parties often must form coalitions—agreements or alliances—with each other.

> Now that they have heard other teams' ideas for new candy bars, ask students to choose one or two teams with similar tastes to their own and form a "coalition" to make a candy bar that members of the new team can all agree upon. What compromises must they make to reach consensus?

What Do You See? (5 minutes)

Read aloud from page 43:

> With a partner, look at how the chairs are arranged in the room in the photo on pages 42 and 43 of your books. The room is the main chamber of the Knesset, Israel's legislature. It was designed to look like a menorah. Do you see it?

Allow students a few moments to see the menorah in the picture. Then, with a partner, have students discuss the questions beneath the photo:

1. Why might the people designing this room have used that shape? *(The menorah, which dates back to Temple times, is a long-standing symbol of the State of Israel and is found on Israel's national emblem.)*
2. In addition to the menorah shape, the chairs are also set up so people can see one another and easily talk. What values do you think led to that decision? *(A democracy is based on the principles of discussion and collaboration. This format allows for all representatives to speak on behalf of the people they represent.)*

See-Think-Wonder: Freedom Posters for Israel (20 minutes)

Say to students:

> In 1943, in the middle of World War II, the U.S. artist Norman Rockwell created a series of paintings celebrating the rights for which Americans were fighting. Called *The Four Freedoms*, the series depicts *Freedom of Speech*, *Freedom of Worship*, *Freedom from Want*, and *Freedom from Fear*. Take a look at the paintings on page 43 of your books.

Tell me what you SEE. *(Answers might include: I see people listening to a man standing and talking; I see a big family meal; I see kids getting tucked in.)*

Look again. What do you THINK might be happening? What do you THINK about when looking at these paintings? *(Answers might include: I think people are listening to each other with respect; knowing these paintings were made during a time of war, I think people are praying for peace.)*

What do you WONDER—what questions do you have? *(Answers might include: I wonder why some people are praying with their eyes closed and others open; I wonder why the dad is holding a newspaper.)*

Teacher Tip: The goal is to help students think about the concept of freedom, to consider what it means, and then to visualize freedom. If students are struggling to come up with questions, prompt their thinking by sharing your own answers to these questions.

Continue:

> Now, pick one of these paintings, and reimagine it by illustrating the same concept using Israeli (not North American) imagery and modern symbols instead of those from the 1940s. Sketch your ideas at the bottom of page 43. Create an actual poster on poster board, using markers, paints, or collage materials. *(Possible adaptations to the imagery might include people wearing kippot, serving Israeli food like falafel and shawarma, praying in a synagogue or at the Kotel; freedom from fear might include a picture of IDF soldiers protecting Israel.)*

Teacher Tip: Try to ensure that all four freedoms are covered. Encourage students to consider what they've learned about diversity in Israel and how that could be reflected in one of these freedom posters.

Allow students time to work on their projects. Once they are finished, encourage them to fill out the artist statement in their books.

Teacher Tip: If time permits, students can hang their posters around the room and see what their classmates have done. Or, check with your education director or principal about hanging these in the hallway and encouraging parents and other students to view the posters.

Do You Disagree? (10 minutes)

Read as a class "Disagreement at the Knesset" on page 45 of the student book. Then, hang up two signs on opposite walls of the classroom: "Agree" and "Disagree." Ask four volunteers to each read aloud one of the statements on page 45:

- I want to visit Israel as soon as possible.
- Israel is a Jewish country.
- Israel is a diverse country.
- Praying at the Kotel would be meaningful to me.

Instruct students that after each statement is read, they should move near the sign that best describes their feelings about that statement—the closer to the sign, the stronger the agreement or disagreement.

When everybody is in place, ask a student who is close to each sign to explain his or her position on the subject. After everyone has heard the two explanations, invite them to reposition themselves in relationship to the signs. Repeat the activity with each of the four statements, then discuss as a class the following questions, found on page 45 of *Israel...It's Complicated.*

1. How did it feel when you heard opinions different than your own? *(It was frustrating that we were not on the same page. It was interesting to see different perspectives.)*

2 Did any of the arguments convince you to reposition yourself? If so, why? If not, why not? *(Yes, because they made me think about the issue in a different way or raised a point that never would have occurred to me. No, because I already felt very strongly about the issue.)*

3 Which statement got the largest range of responses? In what ways did that affect your own ideas about the statement? *(Answers will vary based on class interests, but students might have been swayed by seeing how many or how few of their classmates agreed with them on a specific issue.)*

4 How do you think having debate and disagreement within the Knesset might be helpful for Israel's government? How might it be harmful? *(Debate and disagreement allow for a variety of thoughts and opinions to be heard. Debate and disagreement help ensure that the needs of as many different people as possible are represented. Debate and disagreement might be harmful if people are not willing to listen to the other side but simply focus on making sure their own needs are met.)*

Building Activity: Comparing Governments

Distribute copies of Comparison of Governments, found on page 75 of this guide. In small groups, have students compare some of the ways the Israeli Knesset is similar to and different from either the US Senate and House of Representatives or the Canadian Senate and House of Commons. How does representation differ? How does the election process work? What are some of the advantages and disadvantages of each? Then, invite volunteers to share what they learned with the rest of the group.

Teacher Tip: There is more similarity between Canada and Israel than between the United States and Israel. Indeed, the Israeli system will probably be easier for Canadian students to understand than for their U.S. counterparts. Canada has a parliamentary system, where most political power is concentrated in the legislature, without the "check and balance" of an independently elected president. The prime minister is chosen from among the members of parliament. There is a governor general appointed by the Queen of England, but those powers are limited and that person is not a chief executive in the same way as the president of the United States. That role is more similar to the president of Israel.

Chapter 4 Lesson 2
A Jewish State

Essential Question: How do Jewish values shape the State of Israel?

Learning Objectives: Students will be able to:

- Identify some of the diverse Jewish practices in Israel.
- Articulate some of the challenges raised by Orthodox control of Jewish practice.
- Discuss the rights of women to pray at the Kotel from the perspectives of Women of the Wall and the ultra-Orthodox.

Materials:

"Whose Kotel Is It Anyway?" source sheet

Activities

Getting Started: The First Amendment (10 minutes)

Write on the board:

> Congress shall make no law respecting an establishment of religion, or prohibiting the free exercise thereof; or abridging the freedom of speech, or of the press; or the right of the people peaceably to assemble, and to petition the Government for a redress of grievances.

As students walk into the room, explain that this is the First Amendment to the US Constitution. In pairs, have students discuss what the First Amendment tells us about the role of religion in the United States. *(Possible answers: There is a separation of church and state. There can be no national religion. All people can practice their religion how they best see fit.)*

Then, invite one or more volunteers to read aloud "Which Kind of Jewish?" on page 46 of *Israel... It's Complicated.*

Ask students:

> What questions do you imagine might come up as a result of Orthodox control of Jewish practice in Israel? *(Answers might include: Do restaurants have to be kosher? Can stores sell non-kosher food? Who is Jewish? Do both parents have to be Jewish for their children to be Jewish? Is everybody required to observe Shabbat? Can theaters show movies on Shabbat? If you are Jewish, do you have to marry somebody who is Jewish?)*

Q&A (15 minutes)

Place three chairs at the front of the room, and invite three students, playing Ya'akov, Sarah, and Mosheh, to act out the skit on page 47 of their books. Then, as a class, discuss the questions at the bottom of the page:

1. How would you answer each of Ya'akov's questions? How are your answers similar to or different than those of Mosheh and Sarah? *(Students might agree with either Mosheh or Sarah's answers to each of the questions. They might have difficulty understanding one of the sides, since their experiences are likely different than those of many Israelis.)*
2. What do their answers tell you about life in Israel? *(It was interesting to see just how different their perspectives are from each other. I can't imagine buses not running on Shabbat, but I can understand why Mosheh might want that to happen. I can understand why Sarah might be frustrated that Orthodox values, which she does not agree with, are limiting her choices for how she lives her life. I would be frustrated if someone was trying to tell me how to dress. I am disappointed that some Israelis are choosing not to serve in the Israeli army, as that increases the burden for everyone else.)*
3. What other questions would you want to ask Mosheh and Sarah? How do you think they would answer? *(Students might want to know more about their lives, what helped to shape their perspectives, or how they feel compromises can be better reached between different groups.)*

Building Activity: Freedom, Justice, and Peace

Say to students:

> In the United States, the head of government is the president. In Canada and in Israel, the head of government is the prime minister. Imagine you are the prime minister of Israel and are giving a speech about uniting Israeli Jews to live peacefully and respectfully with each other. How could you include the ideas in the excerpt from Israel's Declaration of Independence at the bottom of page 42 for inspiration? Write a short speech of two to three minutes in length.

Invite volunteers to deliver their speeches to the class. You may wish to film the speeches and upload them to your class website or email a link to parents.

What Happens When Values Conflict? It's Complicated (15 minutes)

Tell students you're going to learn about a group called Women of the Wall (WOW). Invite volunteers to take turns reading aloud "What Happens When Values Conflict" on page 48 of their books.

Then, have students pair up with a friend and negotiate how to work out this issue. One person should represent the concerns of the ultra-Orthodox; the other should represent Women of the Wall. Tell students:

> *Your challenge is to negotiate an agreement that best satisfies the competing needs of both parties.*

Students can begin by listing the main concerns of both sides on the chart on page 49 of their books. *(The ultra-Orthodox may feel that it is disrespectful for women to hold their own services and read from the Torah; they may not want to expose their children to something that goes against their values; they may feel that WOW show a disregard for ultra-Orthodox values; they may wish to avoid conflict at the Kotel, etc. The WOW may feel that it is important to ensure equal rights for women, to avoid discrimination, to set a good example for future generations, to protest overall Orthodox control of how Israelis can practice Judaism, etc.)*

Teacher Tip: Hand out copies of the "Whose Kotel Is It Anyway?" source sheet and encourage students to discuss these Jewish texts in light of WOW and the ultra-Orthodox. Students may use these texts to help bolster their negotiations.

Give students a chance to conduct their negotiation, then ask them to complete the questions on the bottom left of page 49 and share their answers with the class:

- After negotiation, what was the agreement that you came to?
- In what way did it satisfy each party?
- In what way did it disappoint each party?

Reflections: Talk about It! (10 minutes)

As a class, discuss the following questions:

1. How does having a government and society with so many differing opinions make Israel a stronger nation? A weaker one? *(Countries are strengthened when the voices of many are taken into account, when different perspectives allow for the needs of as many people as possible to be met. If those conflicts are not handled respectfully, it can lead to internal conflict and present many challenges for how people interact with one another.)*
2. How would you feel about the religious laws if you lived in Israel? How do you think the laws might affect your life? *(Some students might understand the importance of meeting the needs of the religious. In North America, for example, kosher food is served, and the laws of Shabbat are observed at many communal events to ensure that everyone feels welcome. Some students might express frustration or even anger at the idea of someone else controlling how they practice their Judaism or judging what they wear. It would be limiting not to be able to visit friends or go out to dinner because it was Shabbat. It would be very painful not to be able to marry someone because of religious differences.)*
3. How might Israel be different if it didn't have democratic values? If it didn't have Jewish values? *(Without democratic values, it wouldn't be possible for the needs of so many different types of people to be heard. Without Jewish values, Israel would be like any other democracy—and not the Jewish state.)*

Additional Resources

The following activities and information can supplement the lessons or be used on their own to enrich learning about Israel as a Jewish democracy.

Comparison of Governments

	USA	Canada	Israel
Executive	President elected directly by the people; is head of government.	Governor-general appointed by the King/Queen of England. Head of government is prime minister, head of largest party in parliament.	President elected by the Knesset (parliament). Head of government is prime minister, head of largest party in parliament.
Legislature	Senate—2 elected per state; House of Representatives—435 members elected by districts.	Senate—105 members chosen by governor-general; House of Commons—380 members elected by districts.	Knesset—only one house—120 members representing parties, elected by whole country.
Judicial	Supreme Court can reject laws made by legislators.	Supreme Court can reject laws made by legislators.	Supreme Court can reject laws made by legislators.

—From *CHAI Israel Strand Curriculum Core*, URJ Press.

The Basic Laws, Explained
(Israel's constitution)

The Existing Basic Laws: Summary

- Basic Law: The Knesset (1958)
- Basic Law: Israel Lands as Basic Law: The People's Lands (1960)
- Basic Law: The President of the State (1964)
- Basic Law: The State Economy (1975)
- Basic Law: The Army (1976)
- Basic Law: Jerusalem, the Capital of Israel (1980
- Basic Law: The Judiciary (1984)
- Basic Law: The State Comptroller (1988)
- Basic Law: Human Dignity and Liberty (1992)
- Basic Law: Freedom of Occupation (1994)
- Basic Law: Israel—the Nation State of the Jewish People (2018)

Basic Law: The Knesset

Passed on February 12, 1958 by the third Knesset.

The law does not define the powers of the Knesset, but states that it is the house of representatives of the state, that its seat is in Jerusalem and that upon election it should include 120 members. The law then deals with the electoral system, the right to vote and be elected, the Knesset's term of office, the principles relating to the Knesset elections, the service of Knesset members, the parliamentary immunity of the Knesset members and the Knesset buildings and well as the work of the Knesset and its committees. Article 4 of the law, which states that the system of electing the Knesset members can only be amended by a majority of 61 Knesset members, and article 44, which prevents the amendment of the law by means of the Emergency Regulation, can only be amended by a majority of 80 Knesset members. Amendment No. 9 of the law, which was passed on July 31, 1985, states that a list may not participate in the elections if there is in its goals or actions a denial of the existence of the State of Israel as the state of the Jewish people, a denial of the democratic nature of the state, or incitement to racism. Amendment No. 12, which was passed on February 12, 1991, limits the freedom of Knesset members to move from Parliamentary Group to Parliamentary Group in general, and in return for material benefits in particular.

Basic Law: Israel Lands

Passed on July 25, 1960 by the fourth Knesset.

The basis of the law is the special relationship between the People of Israel and the Land of Israel and its redemption. The law ensures that the state lands, which constitute about 90% of the lands in the state, should remain national property. The law prohibits the transfer of ownership over lands owned by the state, the Development Authority or the Jewish National Fund, either by sale or by any other means, with the exception of types of land or transactions that have been specified in the law.

Basic Law: The President of the State

Passed on June 16, 1964 by the fifth Knesset.

The law was basically a re-enactment of previous instructions which were scattered in other laws. It deals with the status of the President of the Stare, his election (by the Knesset), his qualifications and powers, and the procedures of his work.

Basic Law: The State Economy

Passed on July 21, 1975 by the eighth Knesset.

The law lays down the framework for the budget laws and the basic rule, according to which no taxes, compulsory loans, other compulsory payments and fees may be imposed, or their rates changed, except by law or in accordance with it. Regulations imposing compulsory payments are subject to the approval of the Knesset or one of its committees. In addition, the law deals with the authority to reach agreements involving state assets, the acquisition of rights and the undertaking of obligations in the name of the state, the state budget and its formulation, the printing of bank-notes and the minting of coins. The law also states that: "the state economy is subject to the control of the State Comptroller."

Basic Law: The Military

Passed on March 31, 1976 by the eighth Knesset.

Until the *Basic Law* was passed, the constitutional and legal basis for the operation of the Israel Defense Forces was to be found in the IDF Ordinance of 1948. The *Basic Law* follows the said ordinance, adding instructions regarding the subordination of the military forces to the government, the status of the Chief of Staff, and other instructions on issues dealt with by the Agranat Commission which investigated the circumstances for the outbreak of the Yom Kippur War. The law states that the IDF is the army of the state, and inter alia deals with the compulsory military service and enlistment, as well as the instructions of the army and its orders. It states that "outside the Israel Defense Forces no armed force is to be set up or maintained, except in accordance with the law."

Basic Law: Jerusalem, the Capital of Israel (1980)

Passed on December 13, 1980, by the Ninth Knesset.

The intention of the law is to establish the status of Jerusalem as the capital of Israel and secure its integrity and unity. It determines that Jerusalem is the seat of the President of the State, the Knesset, the Government and the Supreme Court. The law also deals with the status of the holy sites, secures

The Basic Laws, Explained (continued)

the rights of people of all religions, and states that Jerusalem shall be given special priority in the activities of the authorities of the State so as to further its development in economic and other matters.

Basic Law: The Judiciary (1984)

Passed on February 28, 1984, by the Tenth Knesset.
The law establishes the authority of the courts in criminal and disciplinary proceedings, as well as the independence of the judiciary and the openness of judicial proceedings. It also determines the procedures for the appointment of judges. The law includes an instruction regarding its permanence and protection from changes by means of emergency regulations.

Basic Law: The State Comptroller (1988)

Passed on February 15, 1988, by the Twelfth Knesset.
The law, a collection of instructions which had previously been scattered in other laws, determines the powers, tasks and duties of the State Comptroller, who also functions as Ombudsman. It also determines the manner in which the State Comptroller is elected and states that he/she is responsible solely to the Knesset.

Basic Law: Human Dignity and Liberty (1992)

Passed on March 17, 1992, by the Twelfth Knesset.
The law determines that the basic human rights in Israel are based on the recognition of the value of the human being, the sanctity of his life, and his being a free person. The purpose of the law is to protect human dignity and liberty, in order to anchor the values of the State of Israel as a Jewish and democratic state, in a basic law. The law defines human freedom in Israel as being the right to leave the country and enter it, as well as the right to privacy and intimacy, refrainment from searches relating to one's private property, body and possessions, and avoidance of violations of the privacy of one's speech, writings and notes. Violations of the dignity or freedom of man is permitted only in accordance with the law. The law includes an instruction regarding its permanence and protection from changes by means of emergency regulations.

Basic Law: Freedom of Occupation (1994)

The law was passed in its original version on March 3, 1992, by the Twelfth Knesset.

The second version of the law was passed on March 9, 1994, by the Thirteenth Knesset. The law established the right of every citizen or inhabitant to engage in any occupation, profession or trade unless a law which corresponds to the values of the State of Israel, and which serves an appropriate purpose, determines otherwise. The law includes an instruction regarding its permanence and protection from changes by means of emergency regulations. Only a majority of at least 61Knesset members can amend the law. However, the text states that the Knesset may pass a regular law that violates the freedom of occupation, with a majority of at least 61 Knesset members, if it explicitly states that it is valid "despite what is stated in this Basic Law." The validity of such a law shall expire at the end of four years from its inception, unless an earlier date was prescribed in it.

Basic Law: Israel - the Nation State of the Jewish People

Passed on July 19, 2018, by the Twentieth Knesset.

The law determines, among other things, that the Land of Israel is the historical homeland of the Jewish people; the State of Israel is the nation state of the Jewish People, in which it realizes its natural, cultural, religious and historical right to self-determination; and that exercising the right to national self-determination in the State of Israel is unique to the Jewish People. The law also deals with the State's symbols and official language, the status of Jerusalem, the State's connection with the Jewish People and the Ingathering of Exiles.

Source: The State of Israel, Knesset.gov

How Israeli Elections Work

The Election Process: Background

National elections to the Knesset, Israel parliament, are held once every four years, unless circumstances call for early elections. The framework of the Israeli electoral system is defined in Article 4 of the *Basic Law: The Knesset,* which states:

"The Knesset shall be elected by general, national, direct, equal, secret and proportional elections, in accordance with thee Knesset Elections Law."

- *General*: On election day, voters cast one ballot for a political party to represent them in the Knesset. Every Israeli citizen aged 18 or older has the right to vote.
- *National*: The entire country constitutes a single electoral constituency.
- *Direct*: The Knesset, the Israeli parliament, is elected directly by the voters, not through a body of electors.
- *Equal*: All votes cast are equal in weight.
- *Secret*: Elections are by secret ballot.
- *Proportional:* The 120 Knesset seats are assigned in proportion to each party's percentage of the total national vote. However, the minimum required for a party to win a Knesset seat is 2 percent of the total votes cast.

Knesset elections are based on a vote for a party rather than for individuals, and the many political parties that compete for election to the Knesset reflect a wide range of outlooks and beliefs.

The task of forming a government and heading it as prime minister is assigned by the president to the Knesset member considered to have the best chance of forming a viable coalition government in light of the Knesset election results. (The president of the state is elected by the Knesset, every five years; this is mostly a ceremonial job, and the president doesn't have an important role in governing the country.)

Every citizen aged 21, or older is eligible to be elected to the Knesset, provided they have no criminal record and do not hold an official position.

Knesset seats are assigned in proportion to each party's percentage of the total national vote. The number and order of members entering the new Knesset for each party correspond to its list of candidates as presented for election.

Source: Israel Ministry of Foreign Affairs, "The Election Process: Background." www.mfa.gov.il/MFA/AboutIsrael/History/Pages/FAQ_Elections_Israel.aspx

The Knesset: A Building Coalitions Activity

By Marc Rosenstein

Introduction

Israel has a single-house parliament called the Knesset, with 120 members elected at large. A summary of how the Knesset is elected and how a government is formed appears on page 84. Read the text as a class. Then, review the main content items and make sure the students understand how the proportional system works.

The Activity (25-30 minutes)

In this activity students will simulate the coalition-building process. In order to make decisions—including who will be the prime minister and all the other cabinet ministers (labor, defense, health, education, foreign affairs, etc.)—a majority of votes is needed in the Knesset. Since no one party has ever gotten a majority of the seats in the Knesset, parties must band together, finding enough common values to form a coalition, or alliance, that can command a majority on important decisions. So after each election, the largest party begins to negotiate with various smaller parties to try to form such a coalition, based on mutual compromises; the goal is to put together at least 61 Knesset votes. This activity is a simplified version of the real process.

1. Divide the class into groups and assign each to play the role of one of the political groups mentioned the Coalition Worksheet, found on page 83 of this guide.

2. Read through the directions at the top of the Coalition Worksheet and make sure that students know what they are supposed to do.

3. Give the groups 10 minutes or so to review their party's platform and discuss it among themselves; walk around to monitor that each group understands its positions. Suggest they look at the other parties' platforms, too, to see if they have any natural allies or any parties with which it looks like they could not possibly compromise. Suggest that each group make two lists: one list of their "bottom line" positions on which they refuse to compromise and another list of negotiable items. Point out that being included in the coalition means having your members appointed to positions of power, like cabinet ministers and committee chairpersons, and that your party will have some control over the budget. And point out that if you are a small party but have one issue that is very important to you, you should try at all costs to get in the coalition, so that you can use that issue as your condition for supporting the coalition.

4. Turn the two largest parties "loose" to try to put together support from other parties, or each other, in order to form a coalition. Groups can walk around the room to visit other groups in order to broker coalitions. The coalition needs to agree on certain basic things in order to hold together. Suggest that they focus on these issues:

- Should the government play an active role in helping the "weaker" sectors of society (such as the elderly, unemployed, handicapped, new immigrants) by providing them with financial help?
- Should Israel have laws that enforce Jewish religious observance, for example, making stores close on Shabbat?

5 Remind the parties that the voters voted for them because they believed in their principles. If they compromise too much, they are betraying their trust. On the other hand, if they remain outside the coalition, they have significantly less power to influence what goes on in the country.

6 If the process does not reach resolution by about 10 minutes before the end of the class, stop it any way and move to the next step.

7 Debrief: Have the students discuss as a class what happened in the negotiation. If a coalition was achieved, find out what compromises had to be made. Discuss the students' feelings about such com promises; is it fair for a small party to impose its will on the country by this system? Is it democratic? (Maybe it is democratic in that it can prevent the minority from being simply trampled and ignored.) What is the alternative?

Conclusion

Discuss at least one of the following questions as a class:

- What is the impact of having many parties for people to choose from?
- What is the impact of having a system where you vote for a party, not for a person?
- What are some of the different definitions of a Jewish state, according to the different parties?
- Do you think Israel is a Jewish state? Why?

Source: CHAI Israel Strand Curriculum Core, URJ Press

The Knesset: A Building Coalitions Activity

Coalition Worksheet

Your goal is to try to form a coalition between your group and other groups so that you have at least 61 seats in the Knesset. You will have to negotiate with other groups that share similar positions to yours. What will you be willing to compromise? On what won't you be willing to compromise?

Here is a simplified version of the Knesset elections in 2015, with the key platform elements of each group:

Right *(Likud, Yisrael Beitanu, Jewish Home)*

- No negotiations with the Palestinians until they publicly recognize Israel as a Jewish state; and even then, no returning the heart of the holy land in the West Bank
- Lower taxes on the rich to let the economy grow; the poor and disadvantaged should be motivated to find work

Orthodox *(Shas, United Torah Judaism)*

- No army draft for ultra-Orthodox yeshivah students
- Government funding for private religious schools
- No public transportation on Shabbat

Center *(Kulanu, Yesh Atid)*

- Focus on changing the domestic economy, investing more in the middle class and education and health
- Israel must remain a state with a Jewish majority, and work with Arab neighboring countries on an agreement to ensure long-term security
- Push ultra-Orthodox Jews to work and serve in the army, rather than continue to enjoy welfare benefits and army deferral

Left *(Zionist Union, Meretz)*

- Higher taxes on the rich to support welfare programs for the poor and disadvantaged
- Negotiations with the Palestinians now, toward Israeli withdrawal from the West Bank and a peace treaty
- Equalizing the draft, so that everyone has to serve in the army, including the ultra-Orthodox and Arabs
- No government enforcement of religious laws

Arab *(Joint List)*

- More support for welfare programs that help the poor and disadvantaged
- Negotiations with the Palestinians now, toward Israeli withdrawal from the West Bank and a peace treaty
- More cultural independence for Arabs

The Knesset: A Building Coalitions Activity

Forming the Government

The government (cabinet of ministers) is the executive authority of the state, charged with administering internal and foreign affairs, including security matters. Like the Knesset, the government usually serves for four years, but its tenure may be shortened if the prime minister is unable to continue in office due to death, resignation, or impeachment.

When a new government is to be constituted, the president of the state, after consulting with representatives of the parties elected to the Knesset, assigns the task of forming the government to a Knesset member. This Knesset member is usually the leader of the parry with the largest Knesset representation or the head of the parry that leads a coalition with more than 60 members.

Since a government requires the Knesset's confidence to function, it must have a supporting coalition of at least 61 of the 120 Knesset members. To date, no party has received enough Knesset seats to be able to form a government by itself. That means smaller political parties—and there are more than 25—join together to shape the ruling coalition that forms the Israeli government after the ballots get counted.

Here are the results of the election in 2015:

Name	% of votes	Seats in Knesset
Likud ("together")	23%	30
Zionist Union	19%	24
Joint List	11%	13
Yesh Atid ("there is a future")	9%	11
Kulanu	7%	10
The Jewish Home	7%	8
Shas ("Talmud")	6%	7
Yisrael Beiteinu ("Israel Our Home")	5%	6
United Torah Judaism	5%	6
Meretz ("energy")	4%	5

Source: CHAI Israel Strand Curriculum Core, URJ Press. Election information and results ©Behrman House, 2019.

Whose Kotel Is It?

Source Sheet

1 Why was the second Sanctuary destroyed? In its time they were occupying themselves with Torah, [observance of] laws, and the practice of charity? Because there was hatred without cause.

(Yoma 9b)

2 And Miriam the prophetess, the sister of Aaron, took a timbrel in her hand; and all the women went out after her with timbrels and with dances.

And Miriam sang unto them: "Sing ye to the Lord, for He is highly exalted: the horse and his rider hath He thrown into the sea."

(Exodus 15:20–21)

3 Women, slaves, and minors are exempt from reciting Shema and from [wearing] tefillin; but they are obligated [to recite] the Amidah, [to affix a] mezuzah, and [to recite] Birkat Hamazon.

(Mishnah, Berachot 3:3)

4 In the image of God did God create humankind; male and female created He them.

(Genesis 1:27)

5 These and these are the words of the living God.

(Talmud, Eruvin 13b)

Bookstores Told Not to Release "Harry Potter" on Shabbat

Haaretz

Yishai Wages War on Shops Planning Friday Book Launch

By Shiri Lev-Ari
July 18, 2007

The deputy prime minister and minister of industry, trade and employment, Eli Yishai (Shas party), opposes the launch of the new book in the "Harry Potter" series on Friday night. Yishai said he intends to issue indictments and impose fines on local distributors of the book who violate the Hours of Work and Rest Law.

Yishai called on book stores not to sell the book on Shabbat, and instead to begin selling it Friday morning or postpone its sale until after the Sabbath.

The Steimatzky bookstore chain is planning a major launch for the book this Friday night at the Tel Aviv port. At the rival Tsomet Sfarim chain, the book will be launched at a nighttime event at the Ga'ash branch and will go on sale at other branches Saturday morning.

Yishai said yesterday that "there must be a limit to the desire to be like other nations."

MK Avraham Ravitz (United Torah Judaism party) also criticized the planned sale of books on Shabbat.

"Harry Potter and the Deathly Hallows," which is the seventh and final installment in the series written by J.K. Rowling, will be launched simultaneously around the world on July 21, at 02:01 A.M. Israel time.

A statement from Steimatzky said in response: "Under the agreement with the publisher abroad, the chain is obligated to launch the book in Israel simultaneous to its launch throughout the world."

Chapter 5 It Was Built with Hope

Introduction

Enduring Understanding:

Many Jews acted on their dreams of a Jewish state and a desire to control their own destinies by moving to the land and creating the infrastructure for statehood.

Chapter Overview:

This chapter covers the First and Second Aliyot, and highlights the impact of the Dreyfus Affair on Theodor Herzl. Students will learn about the Zionist movement and the British rule of Palestine. It concludes with the creation of the State of Israel in 1948 and the reactions of Jews and Arabs.

Words to Know:

Eretz Yisrael: the Land of Israel

Haganah: Israel's first nationwide Jewish defense organization; it eventually became the Israel Defense Forces (IDF), Israel's army

"Hatikvah": Israel's national anthem; literally "The Hope"

kibbutz: a cooperative community in which members work and eat together, and even share childcare, as if they were part of one large family

Nakba: the "Catastrophe," the Palestinian name for Israel's Independence Day

Yishuv: the community of Jews living in the land of Israel before the founding of the modern state in 1948

Yom Ha'atzma'ut: Israel Independence Day

Zionism: a movement founded by Theodor Herzl to create a homeland for the Jewish people

Balfour Declaration: a commitment from the British government in 1917 to support a Jewish homeland in Palestine

Chapter 5 Lesson 1

Hope for a Home

Essential Question: How did the Jewish people translate their hope for a country into a reality?

Learning Objectives: Students will be able to:

- Discuss the impact of the Dreyfus Affair on Theodor Herzl.
- Articulate the Jewish hope for a land of their own.
- Explain how early Zionists began laying the foundation for the Jewish state.
- Demonstrate knowledge of the First and Second Aliyot.

Materials:

- Crayons and/or markers
- Materials/kits to make tzedakah boxes (optional)

Activities

Getting Started: What Do You See? (5 minutes)

Say to students:

With a friend, compare the two photos of Rehovot found on page 50 of your books. Then, discuss the questions at the bottom of the page:

1. How would you describe each photograph? (The early picture is of a rural area that is very sparsely populated, with very little in the way of vegetation. The modern picture is of a busy, populated city, surrounded by green landscape.)
2. What do you think it would have been like to live in Rehovot in 1893? How about today? (In 1893, Rehovot was likely an isolated, lonely place to live. There wasn't a lot of infrastructure, and the Jewish community was very small. Today, it is a thriving modern city, with shopping malls, office buildings, and much more.)

The Hope for a Home (10 minutes)

Break students into small groups. Have each group make a list of songs that contain the word hope; songs do not need to be Jewish. Go around the room and ask each group to sing the hope lyrics of the first song on their list. If one group sings a song on another group's list, that group must cross it out. Continue until all groups have finished all the songs on their lists.

Ask students:

1. Why do you think there are so many songs about hope? (People need to believe in a brighter future; hope helps people to cope with difficult times.)
2. How do you think hope sustained the early immigrants to Israel? (Their shared hope gave them strength during challenging times; it helped them work together toward a shared goal or purpose.)
3. How might Israel be different without that hope? (It might not exist at all; it might stop working toward peace with its neighbors; it might not be a leader in innovation and technological advances.)

Building Activity: You Are There

In pairs, have students read the background about the Dreyfus Affair found on page 97 of this guide, or research further online. Pretending that they are newspaper reporters covering the story, ask them to prepare a list of interview questions. What would they like to ask Dreyfus? What would they like to ask the soldiers who worked with Dreyfus? What would they like to ask those at the trial? Imagining the answers, have students draft a news article, which they could share with the rest of the class or post on the bulletin board.

Draw the Dream / Describe the Dream (10 minutes each)

Pick one of the activities below.

Activity 1:

Say to students:

> Imagine that you are one of the original pioneers who came to the Land of Israel. In the space at the top of page 53 of your books, draw a simple outline of a house. Inside the house, write words and draw symbols and colors that represent your new home in Israel. What will your home look like? What will your new home provide that you didn't have in your old country? *(Homes would likely be modest and simple, designed to meet basic needs. The new home might provide more safety than was available in the old country, a sense of working toward a larger purpose of building the land, and friendlier neighbors.)*

Activity 2: In lieu of drawing, students may wish to write a letter home about what it is like to live in Israel and how it is similar to and different than their life before making aliyah.

If time permits, students can share their artwork or letters with the class.

Building Activity: Giving Tzedakah

In this activity, students will have the opportunity to create their own tzedakah boxes. There are instructions online you can use or kits that can be purchased. Discuss the best option with your education director.

In class, tell students:

> In the early years, Israel relied heavily on the support it received from Jews around the world, much of it collected in boxes like the one found in the photograph at the bottom of page 53 of your books. Let's continue the tradition by making our own tzedakah boxes.

When students have completed their tzedakah boxes, ask each student in your class to collect a specific dollar amount in tzedakah money from friends or family members. (Small amounts are fine!) Then, as a class, decide where you'd like the money you raised to go: a specific project in Israel, a local Jewish organization, or a secular non-profit that does work that is important to your students.

Moving Forward (20 minutes)

Ask a volunteer to read aloud the directions for the game Moving Forward at the top of page 55 of the student book. For every question an "immigrant" asks, he or she moves forward three steps. For every obstacle an "immigrant" names, other players must take one step back.

(Examples of questions might include: Where will I get food? How can I find a job? How do we stay safe here? Where will my children go to school? Who will take care of me if I am sick? How can I stay in touch with the loved ones I have left behind? Examples of obstacles might include: competition for scarce resources, lack of employment opportunities, living in a desert, lack of societal infrastructure, limited access to health care.)

Once all students have crossed the room, discuss these questions:

1 How easy or hard was it to come up with questions? With obstacles? *(It might be easy for students to imagine what it would be like to be a new immigrant to Israel. Some students might feel that they don't know enough about immigration or life in Israel to really understand what types of questions a new immigrant might ask.)*

2 How do you think the pioneers felt when faced with obstacles? How might they have responded to those obstacles? *(Pioneers may have felt disheartened, determined to succeed, frustrated, tired, overwhelmed, hopeful, optimistic. They may have responded to those obstacles by working harder, giving up, leaning on one another, inventing new solutions.)*

3 How do you think those early pioneers would feel if they could see the country of Israel today? *(They would feel immensely proud of all the progress that has been made; amazed at modern technology, medical innovations, and much more. They might feel that they deserve some of the credit for how far Israel has come. They might be saddened to learn that there is still strife and unrest in the region.)*

Chapter 5 Lesson 2

Mixed Messages

Essential Question: How can Jews balance their joy on Yom Ha'atzma'ut while acknowledging the many challenges that arose as a result of the creation of the State of Israel?

Learning Objectives: Students will be able to:

- Articulate the mixed messages Great Britain sent to both Arabs and Jews prior to the creation of the State of Israel.
- Discuss the obstacles the White Paper caused for Jews trying to escape Europe during and after the Holocaust.
- Express the perspectives of both Jews and Arabs on the Israeli War of Independence.

Materials:

- *Exodus 1947* clip at bhlink.me/israel5 (optional)
- Israel's Declaration of Independence, found on page 99 of this guide or at bhlink.me/israel5 (optional)
- Video of "Hatikvah" found at bhlink.me/israel5

Activities

Getting Started (5 minutes)

Say to students:

With a partner or in a small group, read the text of the Balfour Declaration found on page 56 of your books. Try to imagine you were a Jew living in 1917. How do you think you might have felt reading this document? What questions or concerns might you have had about what this meant for the Jewish people? *(Many Jews were likely excited about what this document might mean for the possibility of a Jewish state. It might have been hard to imagine that the dream could be a reality. They might have had questions or concerns about what the state might look like or what this declaration might mean for the current safety of the Jewish people.)*

Building Activity: Exodus 1947

Say to students:

> Look at the picture of the ship *Exodus 1947* at the bottom of page 57 of your books. The 1960 movie *Exodus*, starring Paul Newman, highlights the story of this ship and the beginnings of the State of Israel. Let's watch a clip of the movie (bhlink.me/israel5).

After students have watched the clip, ask them how they feel about the scene depicted:

> How do you think the people aboard the ship felt? Would you have made the same choices? Why or why not? *(The people on the ship may have felt determined to fight on behalf of the Jewish people, especially after the devastation they had just experienced in Europe. They might have felt nervous about what a hunger strike would mean, especially for those who were most at risk of becoming ill. Students will likely have varying opinions on whether they would have made the same choices.)*

Building Activity: The Declaration of Independence

Find a translation of Israel's Declaration of Independence at bhlink.me/Israel5 or on page 99 of this guide. Project the document for students to see or print out and distribute copies to the class. Ask students what they find most interesting about the document. What questions do they have?

Today's Hatikvah (20 minutes)

Invite students to watch a video of "Hatikvah" at bhlink.me/israel5 and read the words in English in their books:

As long as in the heart within
A Jewish soul still yearns
And onward, toward the ends of the east
An eye still yearns toward Zion

Our hope is not yet lost
The hope of two thousand years
To be a free people in our land
The land of Zion and Jerusalem

Say to students:

> These inspiring words helped launch a nation. But there are some people who feel that "Hatikvah" no longer meets Israel's needs as a national anthem. The song is about the hope (*hatikvah*) for a Jewish state, but it was written about the hopes the early pioneers had. Modern Israelis' hopes are different.
>
> Imagine that it is your job to create a new anthem for Israel. Write it in the space on page 58 of your books, as a poem or song using the original "Hatikvah" melody. Then, read, chant, or sing your new anthem to the class or your friends.

Teacher Tip: Students may choose to focus their new "Hatikvah" on peace in the Middle East, welcoming people from around the world, sharing sacred space, etc.

Dear Diary, It's Complicated (15 minutes)

Read "Independence Day: Celebrations?" on page 60 of *Israel...It's Complicated*, either aloud as a group or individually. Then have students work in pairs to complete the activity on page 61, following the "Dear Diary" directions found there. After students have finished writing and read each other's entries, come together as a group and ask:

> For those of you who wrote from the Israeli Jewish point of view, what surprised you most about how Palestinian Arabs might feel? For those who wrote from the Palestinian Arab point of view, what surprised you most about the Israeli Jews? Does it make you look at the situation differently? *(Possible responses might include: I was surprised by how upset the Palestinian Arabs felt, how frustrated they were by the Israeli Declaration of Independence, how hopeful they were that war would return the land to them. I was surprised by how excited Israeli Jews were when they heard the Israeli Declaration of Independence, even knowing that war was about to break out; knowing that they were about to go to war and might lose all they had worked for must have been very frightening to the Israeli Jews. The only way to achieve peace is to consider the feelings of people on both sides.)*

Reflections: Talk about It! (5 minutes)

Ask three volunteers to each read one of the questions at the bottom of page 61.

1 What do you think the pioneers from over one hundred years ago would think if they saw Israel today? How might they feel? *(The pioneers might be overwhelmed at the large cities, incredible infrastructure, and unimaginable technology that are now prevalent throughout the State of Israel. They might feel gratified that all of their hard work led to the creation of this extraordinary Jewish country. They might feel sad or discouraged that there is still so much fighting and terrorism, and that so many people are still struggling to survive in Israel as the country grapples with income inequality and poverty.)*

2 Why do you think many Jewish people who live outside of Israel celebrate Yom Ha'atzma'ut? *(The creation of the State of Israel was the fulfillment of the dreams of the Jewish people as a whole, not just those living in the Land of Israel. Even Jews who live outside of Israel often consider Israel their homeland.)*

3 What ritual would you create that Jews could do on Yom Ha'atzmaut to recognize the Nakba while still celebrating Israel's independence? *(Hold discussions with Palestinians to learn how they feel about this day, include a tzedakah project to help Palestinians in need as part of Yom Ha'atzma'ut celebrations, etc.)*

Chapter 5 Lesson 3
Jewish Choices

Essential Question: Why did Zionism emerge in nineteenth-century Europe, and what other choices did Jews have to deal with the challenges they were facing?

Learning Objectives: Students will be able to:

- Identify challenges faced by the Jewish people in Europe during the mid- to late-nineteenth century.
- Recognize some of the different solutions to the challenges encountered by Jews that were being proposed at the time.
- Understand that Zionism was one of many responses to European anti-Semitism and that it was not the most popular or widely agreed upon

Materials:

- Map of world Jewish population in 1850, found on page 107 of this guide
- Map of world Jewish population in 2016, found on page 108 of this guide
- *An American Tail* film excerpt (on Netflix or can be rented from Amazon Prime or YouTube, or a short clip is on bhlink.me/israel5)
- Copies of excerpt from the *Jewish State* by Theodore Herzl, found on page 106 of this guide
- Chart of Jewish immigration to Palestine and the United States 1881-1928, found on page 32 of this guide

Getting Started (15 minutes)

Display the 1850 Jewish population map. With a partner or in small groups, ask students to examine the map and discuss the following:

- What does the map show about where Jews lived in 1850? *(The majority of Jews lived in Europe, especially in eastern and southern Europe. The Jewish population in the United States was very small.)*
- How do you a think a map of Jewish population today would be different? *(Today, most Jews live in either Israel or the United States.)*

Display the pie chart of Jewish world population in 2016. Ask:

- Why do you think there was such a dramatic change in where Jews live between 1850 and today? *(Israel didn't exist as a country in 1850; Jews moved away from Europe to escape anti-Semitism, or in search of a better life; many European Jews were killed in the Holocaust.)*

What Would You Do? (15 minutes)

Show students the opening scene from *An American Tail,* which depicts a pogrom in Russia. Stop the film right after the *pogrom* scene (approximately 8 minutes).

Ask students:

- What did you see? *(A Jewish village in Russia is attacked and burned on Hanukkah.)*
- Who were the characters represented? *(The mice represented the Jews of Russia and the cats represented the Cossacks* [semimilitary people in Russia and the Ukraine who participated in and often instigated pogroms against Jews in Eastern Europe]*)*
- If you were the mouse family, which of the following would you have done after experiencing the pogrom? Your choices could include:
  - Moving to America, as Fievel's family did
  - Staying in Russia and hoping things will improve
  - Staying in Russia and fighting back
  - Working to create a Jewish homeland (By moving to Palestine or by working on this idea where you already live)
  - Changing your religion
  - Something else

Herzl's *The Jewish State* (10 minutes)

Hand out copies of the excerpt from Theodor Herzl's *Jewish State*, published in 1896. As a class, discuss the following questions:

- What is Herzl proposing? *(That Jews be given some land to create their own nation.)*
- Why does Herzl propose this? *(Because Jews are being persecuted wherever they live.)*

Does Herzl suggest a specific location for a Jewish country? *(No. He asks for a piece of land that is large enough to hold the Jewish people and does not mention Israel/Palestine or Jerusalem.)*

Reflections: Choices (15 minutes each)

When faced with the anti-Semitism of the Dreyfus Affair, Theodor Herzl advocated Jewish self-determination, the right of Jews to control their own destiny, in their own land; in *An American Tail,* the Mousekewitz family followed a different path and decided to immigrate to the United States.

Choose one of the activities below. If time permits, do both!

Activity 1: Invite students to write a new scene for *An American Tail*: After the pogrom, two mice argue over what the community should do next, move to America or organize Jews to fight for a country of their own. What are the pros and cons of each plan?

Activity 2: Invite students to write a letter to Theodor Herzl explaining why his plan for Jewish self-determination will work only if the place is the Land of Israel. The letter should discuss the special relationship between the Jewish people and the Land of Israel. Ask students to include evidence that supports this special relationship. *(Such evidence might include that the Land of Israel was the birthplace of the Jewish people, Jews pray facing toward Jerusalem, Jewish holidays were connected to the agricultural cycle of the Land of Israel, we say "Next year in Jerusalem" at the end of the seder, etc.)*

Building Activity: Outcomes

Starting in the 1880s, which of the following choices do students think was the most popular?

- Move to America like the Mousekewitz family
- Fight for Jewish self-determination as proposed by Theodor Herzl
- Stay in Europe and hope things get better

Show students the demographic table of Jewish immigration to Palestine and the US between 1881 and 1928, found on page 32 of this guide. Discuss whether the numbers match their predictions.

Teacher Tip: Explain that while anti-Semitic attacks were factors in pushing Jews to leave Europe, we can see from the number that those who moved to the land of Israel were motivated not only by anti-Semitism but by those who believed in the Jewish right to self-determination or wanted to recreate Jewish life in the Land of Israel. Israel was closer, cheaper to get to, and the Zionist movement was advocating for Jews to move there. Yet, despite this being the greatest period of migration in modern Jewish history, only a few decided to take that journey. America offered a relative guarantee of religious freedom and economic opportunity while the Land of Israel was a far greater unknown. We know from additional sources (not included here) that the majority of those who did undertake the path of going to the Land of Israel were ideologically motivated by Jewish self-determination.

Additional Resources

The following activities and information can supplement the lessons or be used on their own to enrich learning about Israel as a place built on hope.

The Dreyfus Affair

The Dreyfus Affair began in 1894 when Alfred Dreyfus, a Jewish officer in the French army, was accused of passing secret French military documents to the German embassy in Paris. Dreyfus was convicted of treason and condemned to life in prison. At first the public supported the conviction; it was willing to believe in the guilt of Dreyfus. Much of the early publicity surrounding the case came from anti-Semitic groups to whom Dreyfus symbolized the supposed disloyalty of French Jews. In 1896, the head of French military intelligence discovered that another French officer was the real traitor, but the evidence was concealed.

Supporters of Dreyfus demanded a new investigation, but opponents insisted Dreyfus and his backers were traitors. Attacks on Dreyfus and the Jewish community were often rooted in anti-Semitic ideas. Journalist Theodor Herzl saw these attacks and this unjust treatment in "enlightened" France, and concluded that anti-Semitism was incurable and that the only place where Jews could be safe was in a state of their own.

Eventually, Dreyfus received a new trial but was found guilty a second time. However, soon after, Dreyfus was pardoned and released, and he was formally exonerated in 1906, when the French Supreme Court annulled his second conviction.

Source: Mitchell Bard, *Israel Matters*, 2015.

The Balfour Declaration

Foreign Office,
November 2nd, 1917.

Dear Lord Rothschild,

I have much pleasure in conveying to you, on behalf of His Majesty's Government, the following declaration of sympathy with Jewish Zionist aspirations which has been submitted to, and approved by, the Cabinet

"His Majesty's Government view with favour the establishment in Palestine of a national home for the Jewish people, and will use their best endeavours to facilitate the achievement of this object, it being clearly understood that nothing shall be done which may prejudice the civil and religious rights of existing non-Jewish communities in Palestine, or the rights and political status enjoyed by Jews in any other country"

I should be grateful if you would bring this declaration to the knowledge of the Zionist Federation.

Source: Wikimedia Commons

Declaration of Independence (Translation)

PROCLAMATION OF INDEPENDENCE

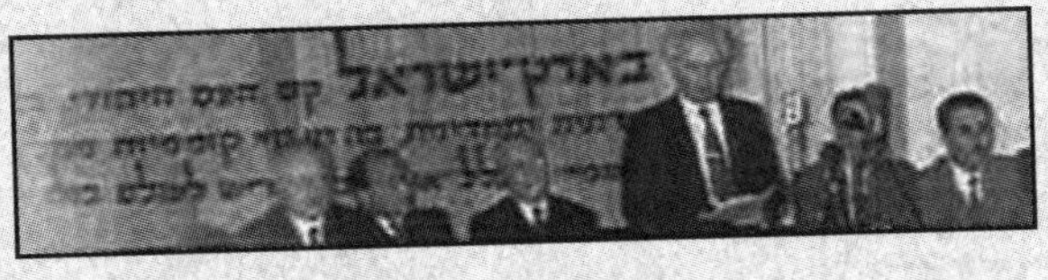

Provisional Government of Israel
Official Gazette: Number 1; Tel Aviv, 5 Iyar 5708, 14.5 1948 Page 1

The Declaration of the Establishment of the State of Israel

The Land of Israel was the birthplace of the Jewish people. Here their spiritual, religious, and political identify was shaped. Here they first attained to statehood, created cultural values of national and universal significance and gave to the world the eternal Book of Books.

After being forcibly exiled from their land, the people kept faith with it throughout their Dispersion and never ceased to pray and hope for their return to it and for the restoration in it of their political freedom.

Impelled by this historic and traditional attachment, Jews strove in every successive generation to re-establish themselves in their ancient homeland. In recent decades, they returned in their mases. Pioneers, defiant returnees, and defenders, they made deserts bloom, revived the Hebrew language, built villages and towns, and created a thriving community controlling its own economy and culture, loving peace, but knowing how to defend itself, bringing the blessings of progress to all the country's inhabitants, and aspiring towards independent nationhood.

In the year 5657 (1897), at the summons of the spiritual father of the Jewish State, Theodore Herzi, the First Zionist Congress convinced and proclaimed the right of the Jewish people to national rebirth in its own country.

This right was recognized in the Balfour Declaration of the 2nd November, 1917, and re-affirmed in the Mandate of the League of Nations, which, in particular, gave international sanction to the historic connection between the Jewish State, which would open the gates of the homeland wide to every Jew and confer upon the Jewish people the status of a fully privileged member of the community of nations.

Survivors of the Nazi holocaust in Europe, as well as Jews from other parts of the world, continued to migrate to Eretz-Israel, undaunted by difficulties, restrictions and dangers, and never ceased to assert their right to a life of dignity, freedom and honest toil in their national homeland.

In the Second World War, the Jewish community of this country contributed its full share to the struggle of the freedom and peace loving nations against the forces of Nazi wickedness and, by the blood of its soldiers and its war effort, gained the right to be reckoned among the peoples who founded the United Nations.

On the 29th November, 1947, the United Nations General Assembly passed a resolution calling for the establishment of a Jewish State in Eretz-Israel; the General Assembly required the inhabitants of Eretz-Israel to take such steps as were necessary on their part for the implementation of that resolution. This recognition by the United Nations of the right of the Jewish people to establish their State is irrevocable.

Declaration of Independence (continued)

This right is the natural right of the Jewish people to be masters of their own fate, like all other nations, in their own sovereign State.

Accordingly, we, members of the People's Council, representatives of the Jewish Community of Eretz-Israel and of the Zionist Movement, are here assembled on the day of the termination of the British Mandate over Eretz-Israel and, by virtue of our natural and historic right and on the strength of the resolution of the United Nations General Assembly, hereby declare the establishment of a Jewish state in Eretz-Israel, to be known as the State of Israel.

We declare that, with effect from the moment of the termination of the Mandate being tonight, the eve of Sabbath, the 6th Iyar, 5708 (15th May, 1948), until the establishment of the elected, regular authorities of the State in accordance with the Constitution which shall be adopted by the Elected Constituent Assembly not later than the 1st October, 1948, the People's Council shall act as a Provisional Council of State, and its executive organ, the People's Administration, shall be the Provisional Government of the Jewish State, to be called "Israel."

The State of Israel will be open for Jewish immigration and for the Ingathering of the Exiles; it will foster the development of the country for the benefit of all its inhabitants; it will be based on freedom, justice and peace as envisaged by the prophets of Israel; it will ensure complete equality of social and political rights to all its inhabitants irrespective of religion, race or sex; it will guarantee freedom of religion, conscience, language, education and culture; it will safeguard the Holy Places of all religions; and it will be faithful to the principles of the Charter of the United Nations.

The State of Israel is prepared to cooperate with the agencies and representatives of the United Nations in implementing the resolution of the General Assembly of the 29th November, 1947, and will take steps to bring about the economic union of the whole of Eretz-Israel.

We appeal to the United Nations to assist the Jewish people in the building up of its State and to receive the State of Israel into the community of nations.

We appeal – in the very midst of the onslaught launched against us now for months – to the Arab inhabitants of the State of Israel to preserve peace and participate in the up building of the State on the basis of full and equal citizenship and due representation in all its provisional and permanent institutions.

We extend our hand to all neighbouring states and their peoples in an offer of peace and good neighbourliness, and appeal to them to establish bonds of cooperation and mutual help with the sovereign Jewish people settled in its own land. The state of Israel is prepared to do its share in a common effort for the advancement of the entire Middle East.

We appeal to the Jewish people throughout the Diaspora to rally round the Jews of Eretz-Israel in the tasks of immigration and up building and to stand by them in the great struggle for the realization of the age-old dream – the redemption of Israel.

Placing our trust in the Almighty, we affix our signatures to this proclamation of this session of the provisional Council of State, on the soil of the Homeland, in the city of Tel-Avis, on this Sabbath eve, the 5th day of Iyar, 5708 (14th May, 1948).

David Ben-Gurion

Daniel Auster
Mordekhai Bentov
Yitzchak Ben Zvi
Eliyahu Berligne
Fritz Bernstein
Rabbi Wolf Gold
Meir Grabovsky
Yitzchak Gruenbaum
Dr. Abraham Granovsky
Eliyahu Dobkin
Meir Wilner-Kovner
Zerach Wahrhaftig
Herzl Vardi
Rachel Cohen
Rabbi Kalman Kahana
Saadia Kobashi
Rabbi Yitzchak Meir Levin
Meir David Loewenstein
Zvi Luria
Golda Myerson
Nachum Nir
Zvi Segal
Rabbi Yehuda Leib Hacohen Fishman
David Zvi Pinkas
Aharon Zisling
Moshe Kolodny
Eliezer Kaplan
Abraham Katznelson
Felix Rosenblueth
David Remez
Berl Repetur
Mordekhai Shattner
Ben Zion Sternberg
Bekhor Shitreet
Moshe Shapira
Moshe Shertok

Source: The State of Israel, knesset.gov

Deciphering the Declaration: An Activity

By Richard Walter

In this activity, students will work with a primary source—Israel's Declaration of Independence—to Identify key phrases and concepts in the document and differentiate between intentions and outcomes.

Getting started: Begin by asking students what a Declaration of Independence is. *(A document that announces a group's intention to form an independent body such as a country. It usually outlines the group's reasons for seeking this change and often will lay out a vision for the new entity.)*

Next, ask students to imagine that it is May 1948 and they have been asked to join the committee which is writing a Declaration of Independence for a new Jewish state.

> *What do they think are some key phrases or ideas for a Declaration of Independence of a Jewish and Democratic state?* (protection from anti-Semitism, Jewish holidays as public days, freedom of religion, equality for women, etc.)

After they have compiled their lists, distribute the word cloud of Israel's Declaration of Independence (found on following page). What terms were similar or different? What do they notice about the words that appear largest in the word cloud?

Analyze the text: Divide students into small groups and distribute the template and a sheet of labels (found on the following pages) to each group. Explain that they will be creating their own visual analysis of Israel. Working in small groups, have students choose the 2–4 key phrases from the sheet of labels that they feel are most important in terms of what Israel represents for them or as a Jewish and democratic state. They should stick (if using labels, otherwise use tape or glue) them into the box on the blank template found on the following pages. If they wish to add additional questions or comments about the phrases they chose, they can do so in the box. *(Note: The key phrases are best printed on labels Avery 5160 labels.)*

Commentary: After each group has completed their page, have each group pass their page to another group, who should add additional commentary and questions outside the box. Allow for at least two passes and then return the pages to their original groups.

Discuss: Why did they choose the phrases that they did? Why do they think these phrases were included in Israel's Declaration of Independence? What were some of the similarities and differences between the groups? What questions or comments did they add to other group's pages?

Drawing Parallels: Distribute copies of the Tractate Israel template, found on the following pages. Explain that the activity they just completed about the Declaration is similar to what ancient scholars did years ago that resulted in the Talmud, the collection of oral and written Jewish laws and rabbinic discussions. This is an example of a section of the Talmud, called a "tractate."

Just as the Talmud is a record of debate and discussion on matters important to Judaism and Jewish law and observance, Israel is an issue that we can also continually debate and discuss.

Word Cloud: Israel's Declaration of Independence

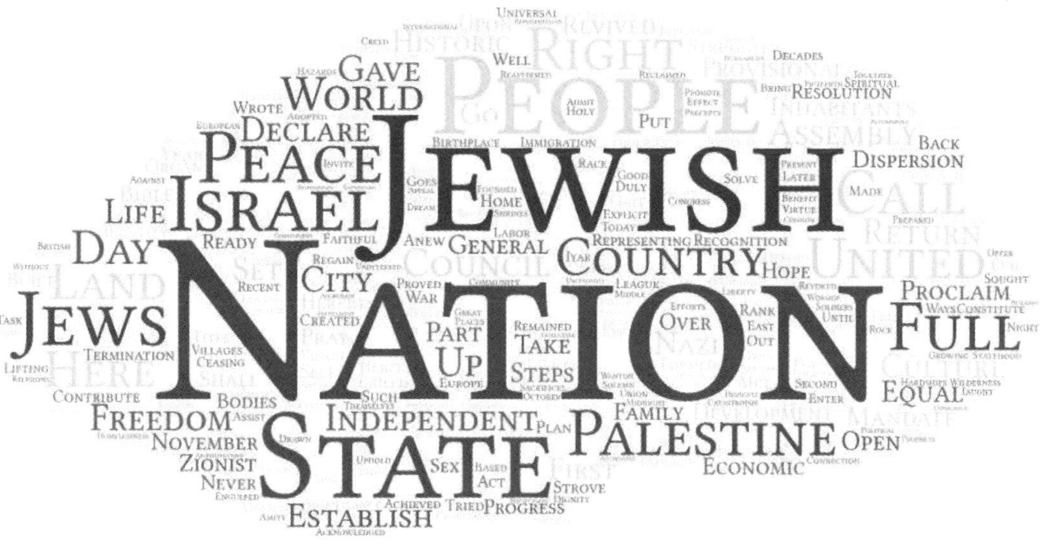

Talmud: Sample Tractate

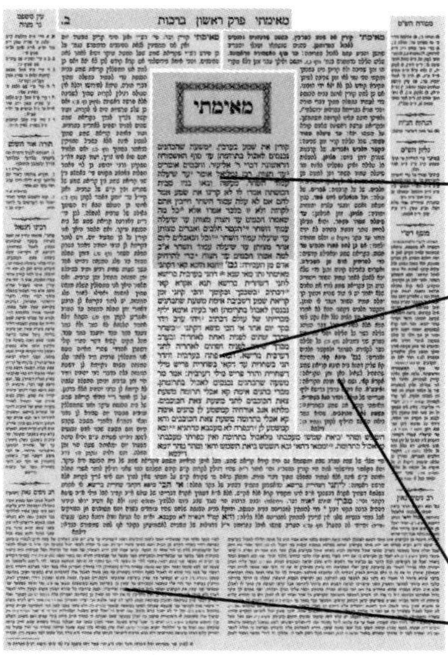

A tractate is a section of the Talmud, the collection of oral and written Jewish laws and rabbinic discussions.

A traditional page of Talmud has several elements:

The Mishnah—the oral law that was first written in Jerusalem in 200 CE.

The Gemara—a collection of discussions on the Mishnah held by various rabbis between 200 CE and 500 CE. There were actually two editions of the Gemara. The first was compiled in Jerusalem (Jerusalem Talmud) around 400 CE and the second was compiled in Babylonia (Babylonian Talmud, or usually just the Talmud) about 100 years later. Together the Mishnah and Gemara make up the Talmud.

Rashi and Tosafot commentaries—Notes and discussions on the Mishnah and Gemara by Rashi, an 11th century French rabbinic scholar and the Tosafot (literally meaning additions), other leading scholars from the 12th and 13th centuries.

Source: ©Center for Israel Education, 2018

Deciphering the Declaration: An Activity (continued)

My Tractate Israel

Key Phrases from Israel's Declaration of Independence

(Note: for best results, print on labels Avery 5160 labels.)

The birthplace of the Jewish People	It will ensure complete equality of social and political rights to all its inhabitants irrespective of religion, race or sex	This right is the natural right of the Jewish people to be masters of their own fate, like all other nations, in their own sovereign State.
Here their spiritual, religious and political identity were shaped	It will guarantee freedom of religion, conscience, language, education and culture.	The State of Israel will be open for Jewish immigration and for the Ingathering of the Exiles.
It will safeguard the holy places of all religions.	The people kept faith throughout their dispersion and never ceased to pray and hope for their return.	It will be based on freedom, justice and peace as envisaged by the prophets of Israel.
Placing our trust in the [Rock of Israel].	In 5657 (1897) the First Zionist Congress . . . proclaimed the right of the Jewish people to national rebirth.	It will take steps to bring about the economic union of the whole of Eretz Israel
	[The right to rebuild a national home] was recognized in the Balfour Declaration of the 2nd November 1917.	We appeal . . . to the Arab inhabitants of the State of Israel to preserve peace and participate in the upbuilding of the State on the basis of full and equal citizenship.
	The massacre of millions of Jews in Europe was another clear demonstration of the urgency of solving the problem of its homelessness.	We extend our hands to all neighbouring states and their peoples in an offer of peace and good neighbourliness.
	On the 29th November, 1947, the United Nations General Assembly passed a resolution calling for the establishment of a Jewish State in Eretz Israel.	We appeal to the Jewish people throughout the Diaspora to rally round of the Jews of Eretz Israel in the tasks of immigration and upbuilding.

Source: ©Center for Israel Education, 2018

Excerpt from Theodor Herzl's *Jewish State*, published in 1896

"No one can deny the gravity of the situation of the Jews. Wherever they live in perceptible numbers, they are more or less persecuted....

I shall now put the Question in the briefest possible form: Are we to "get out" now and where to? Or, may we yet remain? And how long?...

The whole plan is in its essence perfectly simple, as it must necessarily be if it is to come within the comprehension of all.

Let the sovereignty be granted to us over a portion of the globe large enough to satisfy the rightful requirements of a nation; the rest we shall manage for ourselves."

Image courtesy of Wikimedia Commons

Source: Herzl, Theodor. "The Jewish Question." *The Jewish State*. Trans. Sylvie D'Avigdor. 1896. N.p.: American Zionist Emergency Council, 1946.

By the Numbers

World Jewish Population, 1850

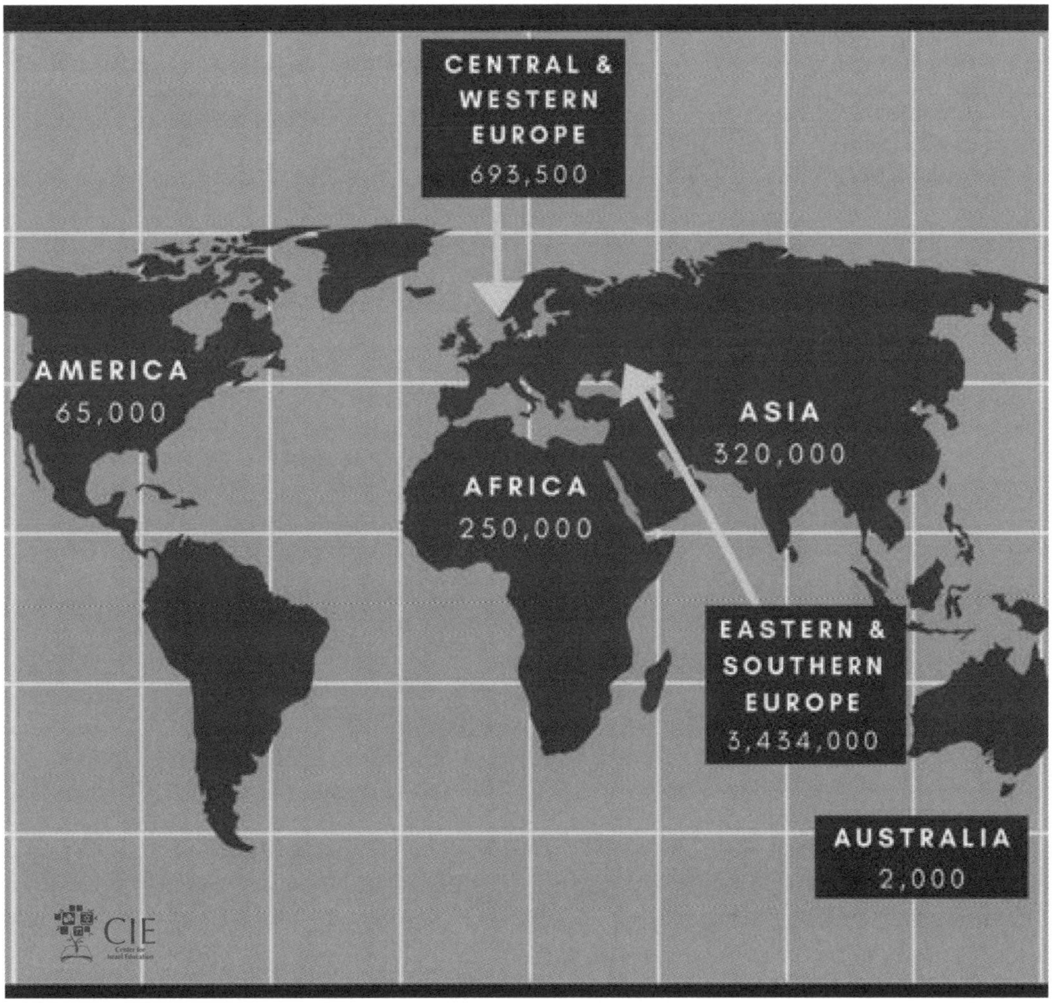

Source: ©Center for Israel Education, 2018

By the Numbers

World Jewish Population, 2016

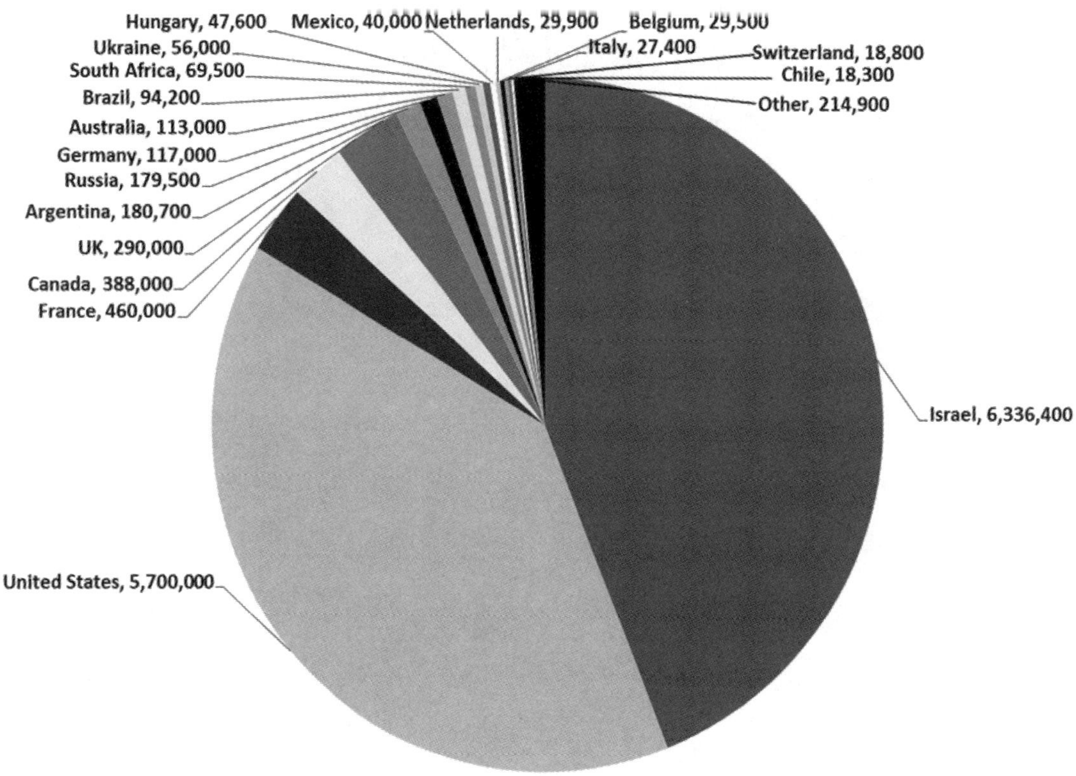

Source: American Jewish Year Book, 2016.

Chapter 6

It's a Place of Conflict in Search of Peace

Introduction

Enduring Understanding:

Conflicts in the Middle East are continuous and complex, with real implications for Israelis in their day-to-day lives. As Israel works toward peace, it must balance the need for security with measures to de-escalate conflict.

Chapter Overview:

This chapter covers Israeli military history and the peace process from 1948 to the present day. Students will learn about the Israel Defense Forces, review a timeline of Israel's wars, and examine critical events in the search for peace. Students will discuss some of the ethical dilemmas associated with Israeli settlements on the West Bank.

Words to Know:

Hamas: formed in 1987 to represent Palestinians; provides everyday services to Palestinians, such as schools and hospitals, and also calls for the destruction of Israel and engages in attacks against Israelis; is considered by many to be a terrorist organization

Israel Defense Forces (IDF): Israel's military; most men and women are required to join at age eighteen.

Palestine Liberation Organization (PLO): a group created by the Palestinians in 1964; its original goals included the destruction of Israel

***piku'ach nefesh*:** "saving a life"; one of the highest values in Judaism

settlements: communities built in the West Bank by Israeli citizens

Two-State Solution: a common suggestion for solving the Israeli-Palestinian conflict; calls for the West Bank and Gaza to separate from Israel and become a separate country called Palestine

Chapter 6 Lesson 1
The IDF, Conflict, and Peace

Essential Question: What conflicts has Israel faced, and how have Israelis continued to work toward peace?

Learning Objectives: Students will be able to:

- Identify some of the conflicts that Israel has experienced since 1948.
- Name key points in the peace process.
- Articulate the IDF's role in keeping Israelis safe and upholding its humanitarian duty to protect civilians on all sides.

Materials:

- markers and/or crayons
- video of *A Day in the Life of the IDF* found at bhlink.me/israel6 (optional)
- video about the Sderot Indoor Playground at bhlink.me/israel6 (optional)

Activities

Getting Started (5 minutes)

With partners or in small groups, have students study the photos and captions on page 62 of *Israel...It's Complicated* and discuss the three questions in "What Do You See?":

1. How do these photos make you feel? *(The top photo makes me sad and scared about the level of violence and hatred that exists between Israelis and Palestinians. The bottom photo makes me hopeful that the two groups can work together for peace.)*
2. What conclusions might you come to about the Israeli-Palestinian relationship based only on the first photo? On the second photo? *(From the top photo, it is hard to imagine a time when we might have peace. From the bottom photo, it appears that the two groups can find things in common, a shared love of music, for example. That might be the first step toward building a meaningful and productive relationship.)*
3. Using both photos as your information source, how would you describe the relationship between Jews and Palestinians in Israel? *(Like a lot of other things discussed in this book—it's complicated. There are many times when Jews and Palestinians are colleagues, neighbors, and even friends. There are many other times when a fiercely adversarial relationship exists.)*

After High School (10 minutes)

Ask:

What are some things you'd like to do after you graduate high school?

Distribute blank paper and markers, and have students draw two pictures, one depicting what they might do when they graduate high school in the US or Canada, and the other imagining that they live in Israel and will be serving in the IDF after high school, as required of most eighteen-year-olds.

After students have completed their drawings, invite them to show their pictures to the class and share their feelings about both possibilities *(The first picture may depict them excitedly or nervously going to college, taking a gap year, traveling abroad, getting a job, missing their families, or even joining the US or Canadian army. Students in Israel might be excited about the prospect of serving in the military on behalf of the State of Israel, living in a new place, making new friends, or gaining new skills and training. They might be frightened about getting hurt or killed, or watching a loved one be hurt or killed. They might be scared about keeping up with the rigorous demands of army life or worried about missing their friends and family at home.)*

Building Activity: A Day in the Life

Show the video *A Day in the Life of the IDF* found at bhlink.me/israel6. Ask students:

What did you find most interesting about the video? Was anything surprising? What does this show you about what life is really like for a soldier in the IDF? *(Students might find the range of activities the soldiers do in a day interesting—everything from physical training to helping people who have been injured, even though the injured are not Israelis. They might be surprised by the strong comradery between the soldiers, who clearly enjoy spending time together, singing and working as a team. Soldiers work hard in preparation for the challenging tasks ahead of them.)*

If you could talk to an IDF soldier, what would you ask him or her? How do you think he or she might respond? *(Students might want to know what the soldiers have learned in their army experiences or whether they object to enlistment being mandatory. Soldiers may share how proud they are to serve their country, their concerns or fears about army life, and how they think army life is preparing them for future careers.)*

Text Study: The Values of the IDF (10 minutes)

Working in pairs, ask students to read and discuss the two texts found on page 63 of their books. Then, pose the following questions to the class:

- The IDF's job is to keep Israel's citizens safe. Do you think the IDF code of ethics makes that job easier or harder? Why? *(In some ways, it makes it easier because IDF soldiers are operating with shared values and intentions for how to do their jobs. It also is easier to make tough decisions when you know you are doing so with the ultimate goal of keeping fellow Israeli citizens safe and protecting all innocent human life. In other ways, the code of ethics makes the job harder: IDF soldiers often are placed in greater danger as they work to protect innocent civilians.)*

- Judaism teaches that piku'ach nefesh, "saving a life," takes precedence over almost anything else. How do you see this value reflected in the IDF's code of ethics? *(The code of ethics instructs soldiers to protect civilians and always to be guided by the supreme value of human life.)*

Building Activity: My Personal Code of Ethics

Say:

> Many companies and organizations—including the IDF, as we've learned—operate under codes of conduct or organizational ethics. People do too. Think of your own personal code of ethics. What are five values that you always try to uphold? *(Examples might include: do not lie, do not cheat, do not use drugs or alcohol, do not gossip, stand with your friends against bullies, ask a trusted adult for help if somebody makes your or your friends feel physically or emotionally uncomfortable.)*

With a partner, have students choose one of the following ethical dilemmas, and discuss what they would do:

1. You're about to take a big history test. No matter how hard one of your good friends studies, she can't remember all the material and is afraid she's going to fail. After the test, she tells you that she cheated, sneaking into the test a slip of paper with names and dates. What does your personal code of ethics tell you to do?
2. Your friend drinks alcohol at a party and looks sick. He goes to bed before his parents get home. You see his mom that next day, and she asks if the two of you had fun at the party. What does your personal code of ethics tell you to do?
3. You buy a new pair of jeans. The salesperson gives you twenty dollars change instead of the ten dollars you were supposed to get. What does your personal code of ethics tell you to do?

Teacher Tip: Ask students to make up their own scenarios or ask each group to create a scenario for another group to discuss.

Explore the Timeline (20 minutes)

Have students study the timeline that begins in their books on page 64. Then instruct students:

- Draw a star next to times when Israel was at war or in a conflict. Draw a circle next to times when steps were taken toward peace. *(Stars: 1948-9 War of Independence, 1956 Suez War, 1967 Six-Day War, 1973 Yom Kippur War, 1982 First Lebanon War, 1987 First Intifada, 2000 Second Intifada, 2006 Second Lebanon War, 2007 Hamas Take-Over of Gaza, 2008 Operation Cast Lead, 2014 Operation Protective Edge.*

  Circles: 1979 Israel-Egypt Peace Treaty, 1991 Madrid Peace Conference, 1993 Oslo Accords, 1994 Israel-Jordan Peace Treaty, 2000 Israel Withdraws from Lebanon, 2000 Camp David Summit, 2005 Israel Withdraws from Gaza.)

- Compare the quotes from Nedal Zahran and Carmit Malka (pages 67 and 68). What concerns do they share? How are their perspectives different? *(Both Nedal and Carmit are concerned for their safety and the safety of their peoples. They are both worried about what the future might hold.*

There may never have been a time when Nedal felt safe and secure where she was living. Carmit worries that her children will not have the same safe childhood that she was able to enjoy.)

- Imagine you are extending the timeline into the future. What possibilities could you imagine between Israel and its neighbors: Will Israel sign new peace treaties? Might there be another intifada? Will Israel ally with neighboring countries to fight a shared enemy? What kinds of new Israeli and Palestinian leaders may emerge? Will the United States or other countries help broker a two-state solution between Israel and the Palestinians? Will technological advances increase the risk of war or the possibility of peace? In the boxes on page 69 write and illustrate what you think will happen in the next five years. The next ten years. The next twenty-five years.

Teacher Tip: In the next lesson, students will learn about Israeli settlements on the West Bank and discuss whether the settlements enhance Israel's security or are obstacles to peace. You may wish to have students hold off on completing the timeline—"What do you think will happen between Israel and its neighbors in the next five years, ten years, and twenty-five years?"—until the end of lesson 2.

Building Activity: Bomb Shelter Playground

Say to the class:

> To help kids like Carmit, the Jewish National Fund built an indoor playground for the children of Sderot. It is built inside a bomb shelter, to help keep the kids safe in case of rocket attacks like the one that destroyed Carmit's home.

Watch the video about the playground (bhlink.me/israel6). Then discuss:

> How do you think the children of Sderot feel when they are playing in this playground? Do you think they can forget why they are playing indoors? How would you feel if you and your friends had to play in a facility like this one?

Building Activity: Help the Kids of Sderot

If you were inspired by the kids in this video, consider helping to fund the program! Work as a class to raise some money to send to JNF to help keep this playground open. You can decide whether you want to use your tzedakah money or hold a fundraising event like a bake or book sale.

Teacher Tip: Check with your education director to follow appropriate fundraising rules for your organization.

Chapter 6 Lesson 2

Do Settlements Promote Security or Conflict? It's Complicated

Essential Question: What role do the West Bank settlements play in the quest for peace and security in Israel?

Learning Objective: Students will be able to:

- Explain the key arguments for and against the West Bank settlements and begin to form their own opinion about the legitimacy, importance, and future of the settlements.

Activities

Getting Started (10 minutes)

Distribute blank paper, and say to the class:

> Imagine that, because of limited resources, your class and another class have to share your classroom. Using paper and pens or pencils, draw a quick sketch of your classroom, including desks or chairs, tables, bookcases, bulletin boards, and other objects in the room. Now, without moving furniture and objects around, draw a line showing how you could share the room.

Ask:

> What obstacles might stand in the way of learning? What are some ways you could work together? What additional challenges might arise if there was a history of conflict between some members of each of the classes? What if each class believed that the classroom space was rightfully theirs and the other group didn't belong?

Invite students to share their thoughts. After the discussion, tell students:

> This activity can give you a glimpse into how challenging it has been for Israelis and Palestinians who are living together in the West Bank.

On Your Feet: West Bank Settlements (10 minutes)

Have students read aloud "Do the Settlements Promote Security or Conflict?" on page 70 of their books. Distribute and have students read the Settlements, Peace, and Security Source Sheet found on page 128 of this guide. Then, say:

> I'm going to read a series of statements to you. When I finish each statement, I want you to stand if you agree with it and remain seated if you disagree. There are no right or wrong answers, so go with your initial response.

After you read each statement, call on one sitting and one standing student to explain their opinions. Once students have heard both sides, students can change their minds, sitting or standing accordingly. Here are the ten statements:

1. All Israeli settlers should leave the West Bank immediately.
2. Israeli settlers have the right to live on the West Bank.
3. Israel should make the Jewish settlements legally part of Israel.
4. Israel should make the entire West Bank legally part of Israel.
5. All of the West Bank, including the Jewish settlements, should be made into a Palestinian state.
6. The Jewish settlement should become part of Israel, and the rest of the West Bank should be a Palestinian state.
7. The status quo of the settlements and the West Bank should remain frozen until it is clear that there will be no rockets or other terrorist attacks launched from the West Bank by Palestinians.
8. Israel should expand and build as many settlements in the West Bank as it wants.
9. If I lived in Israel, I would move to a settlement.
10. If I lived in Israel, I would never visit a settlement.

Debate It! Where to Live? (15 minutes)

Invite a volunteer to read "Debate It!" on page 71:

> Your friend Adi's family is planning to move to Israel. Her dad wants to live in the West Bank because it's more affordable. Her mother thinks Jewish people shouldn't live in the West Bank because it makes the peace process more challenging. Adi doesn't know what to think.

Then ask:

> Should Adi's family move to the settlements?

Working in pairs, thinking about whether the settlements promote peace or conflict and their own feelings about the settlements, have students take a side and debate the issue. Or invite pairs of students to role-play Adi's parents for the class. After listing the main points in their books, discuss the following questions as a group:

- What ethical or moral concerns came up for you as you debated this issue? How did it make you feel? *(Students may worry that every new family moving to the West Bank makes the peace process more difficult. They might be concerned about the safety of Adi's family. They might worry that the rights of Palestinians living in the West Bank are being ignored or violated.)*

- Adi's father wants to live in the West Bank for economic reasons. Would you feel differently about their potential move if he wanted to live on the West Bank for a different reason, such as a religious belief in the Jewish connection to the land or a desire to create positive relationships with Palestinians living there? *(Students might feel that an altruistic reason is a stronger one for moving to the area than an economic one. They might feel that Adi's family has the right to live anywhere they wish, no matter the reason.)*

Building Activity: Go Team!

Say to the class:

> Imagine that Adi lives in a community like ours and attends a school like yours. Over the last few years, Adi's community has welcomed several new immigrant families. Adi and her friends love playing soccer. They invited the children from these immigrant families to join a new soccer league that would bring everybody in the community closer together. Adi hopes that when she and her family move to Israel, she'll be able to join a sports league that includes both Israeli and Palestinian kids, whether or not she lives in the West Bank.
>
> Now imagine that you and your friends wanted to launch a soccer league like Adi and her friends. Think about some of the steps you would need to take to make this happen. Let's start by working as a class on ground rules for the league. What needs to be in place to make this league successful? *(Ground rules might include: respecting individual differences, providing food that is respectful of dietary restrictions, not having games on religious holidays, treating all league members with kindness.)*

Once the class has agreed on a set of ground rules, divide the students into three groups:

1. Creative. Come up with a name for the league. What do you want the name to reflect? Then, design a logo for the league. What image represents the idea behind the league? *(Possible names include: Removing Barriers, All In, One Family, Equality. Name should reflect the importance of everyone being included. The logo might include images like teammates holding a soccer ball, a group of people from a variety of backgrounds, or a globe.)*
2. Fundraising. What are some ways you can help raise funds for uniforms and equipment the teams will need? *(bake sales, car washes, solicit donations from local businesses, babysitting services, coaching younger kids, doing chores in exchange for donations)*
3. Social opportunities. How can you create programs that will help the soccer players and their families get to know one another? *(Have potluck dinners at one another's homes, have coffee meet-ups for parents, create a group on social media that people can follow, play icebreakers before each game.)*

When all the groups have finished, give each group a few minutes to present their ideas to the class. Then ask:

> How do you think a sports program like this could help bring Israeli and Palestinian kids together? Why is that important?

Building Activity: West Bank Bar Mitzvah

Read to students the following story:

> As Yosef prepared to become a bar mitzvah, he looked forward to having his whole family celebrate with him. He had attended the b'nei mitzvah celebrations of many of his cousins, and now it was his turn. But, then, some relatives threatened to boycott his celebration.
>
> Yosef's family lives in a small settlement called Migron, on the Israeli West Bank. It is disputed territory, and some of Yosef's relatives do not think Jews should be living there. These relatives refused to attend Yosef's bar mitzvah, as a political statement. "Their refusal [to come to the bar mitzvah] made me feel a bit miserable," says Yosef. "Like I was a second-class citizen."

Ask the group:

> If you were Yosef, how would you have felt? Why do you think some of Yosef's relatives chose not to attend his celebration?

Based on their understanding of the reading on page 70 and the source sheet, have them work in pairs or small groups to discuss the following questions:

- If you were Yosef, how would you feel about Keifa? Carmit?
- If you were Keifa, how would you feel about Yosef? Carmit?
- If you were Carmit, how would you feel about Keifa? Yosef?

Reflections: Talk about It! (10 minutes)

Ask for a volunteer to read the story of Rabbi Hillel in "Talk about It" on page 71. Then ask students to share their answers to these questions with the class:

Teacher Tip: If you wish, you can encourage students to give their answers while actually standing on one foot. Be mindful of any students with any physical limitations that would prevent them from answering the questions in this way. It might help to advise students to think through their answers carefully before standing on one foot.

1. Imagine someone asked you to explain the conflicts described in this chapter while standing on one foot—in other words, to sum them up very briefly. What would you say? *(The Israeli and Palestinian people both believe they have a historical and religious claim to the land of Israel. As a result, there have been decades of conflict as each group tries to claim ownership of the land.)*
2. How do you think the people who live in the Middle East might benefit from Rabbi Hillel's advice? *(For many people living in the region, there is an undercurrent of distrust and even hatred toward the other group in the conflict. If more work was being done to help reduce hateful or hurtful behavior, there might be a greater chance for peace in the region.)*

If your students have not yet completed the timeline on page 69 of the student book, have them fill in what they think will happen between Israel and her neighbors in the next five years, ten years, and twenty-five years. Invite students to share their predictions with the group.

Additional Resources

The following activities and information can supplement the lessons or be used on their own to enrich learning about Israel as a place of conflict.

United Nations Partition Plan for Palestine

U.N. GENERAL ASSEMBLY

Resolution 181 (II). Future Government of Palestine

29 November 1947

A

The General Assembly,

Having met in special session at the request of the mandatory Power to constitute and instruct a special committee to prepare for the consideration of the question of the future government of Palestine at the second regular session;

Having constituted a Special Committee and instructed it to investigate all questions and issues relevant to the problem of Palestine, and to prepare proposals for the solution of the problem, and

Having received and examined the report of the Special Committee (document A/364)[1] including a number of unanimous recommendations and a plan of partition with economic union approved by the majority of the Special Committee,

Considers that the present situation in Palestine is one which is likely to impair the general welfare and friendly relations among nations;

Takes note of the declaration by the mandatory Power that it plans to complete its evacuation of Palestine by 1 August 1948;

Recommends to the United Kingdom, as the mandatory Power for Palestine, and to all other Members of the United Nations the adoption and implementation, with regard to the future government of Palestine, of the Plan of Partition with Economic Union set out below;

Requests that

(a) The Security Council take the necessary measures as provided for in the plan for its implementation;

1 The Mandate for Palestine shall terminate as soon as possible, but in any case, not later than 1 August 1948.

United Nations Partition Plan for Palestine (continued)

(b) The Security Council consider, if circumstances during the transitional period require such consideration, whether the situation in Palestine constitutes a threat to the peace. If it decides that such a threat exists, and in order to maintain international peace and security, the Security Council should supplement the authorization of the General Assembly by taking measures, under Articles 39 and 41 of the Charter, to empower the United Nations Commission, as provided in this resolution, to exercise in Palestine the functions which are assigned to it by this resolution;

(c) The Security Council determine as a threat to the peace, breach of the peace or act of aggression, in accordance with Article 39 of the Charter, any attempt to alter by force the settlement envisaged by this resolution;

(d) The Trusteeship Council be informed of the responsibilities envisaged for it in this plan;

Calls upon the inhabitants of Palestine to take such steps as may be necessary on their part to put this plan into effect;

Appeals to all Governments and all peoples to refrain from taking action which might hamper or delay the carrying out of these recommendations, and

Authorizes the Secretary-General to reimburse travel and subsistence expenses of the members of the Commission referred to in Part I, Section B, paragraph 1 below, on such basis and in such form as he may determine most appropriate in the circumstances, and to provide the Commission with the necessary staff to assist in carrying out the functions assigned to the Commission by the General Assembly.

B

The General Assembly

Authorizes the Secretary-General to draw from the Working Capital Fund a sum not to exceed $2,000,000 for the purposes set forth in the last paragraph of the resolution on the future government of Palestine.

Hundred and twenty-eighth plenary meeting
29 November 1947

Source: United Nations, www.un.org/unispal

Partition Plan Map (1947)

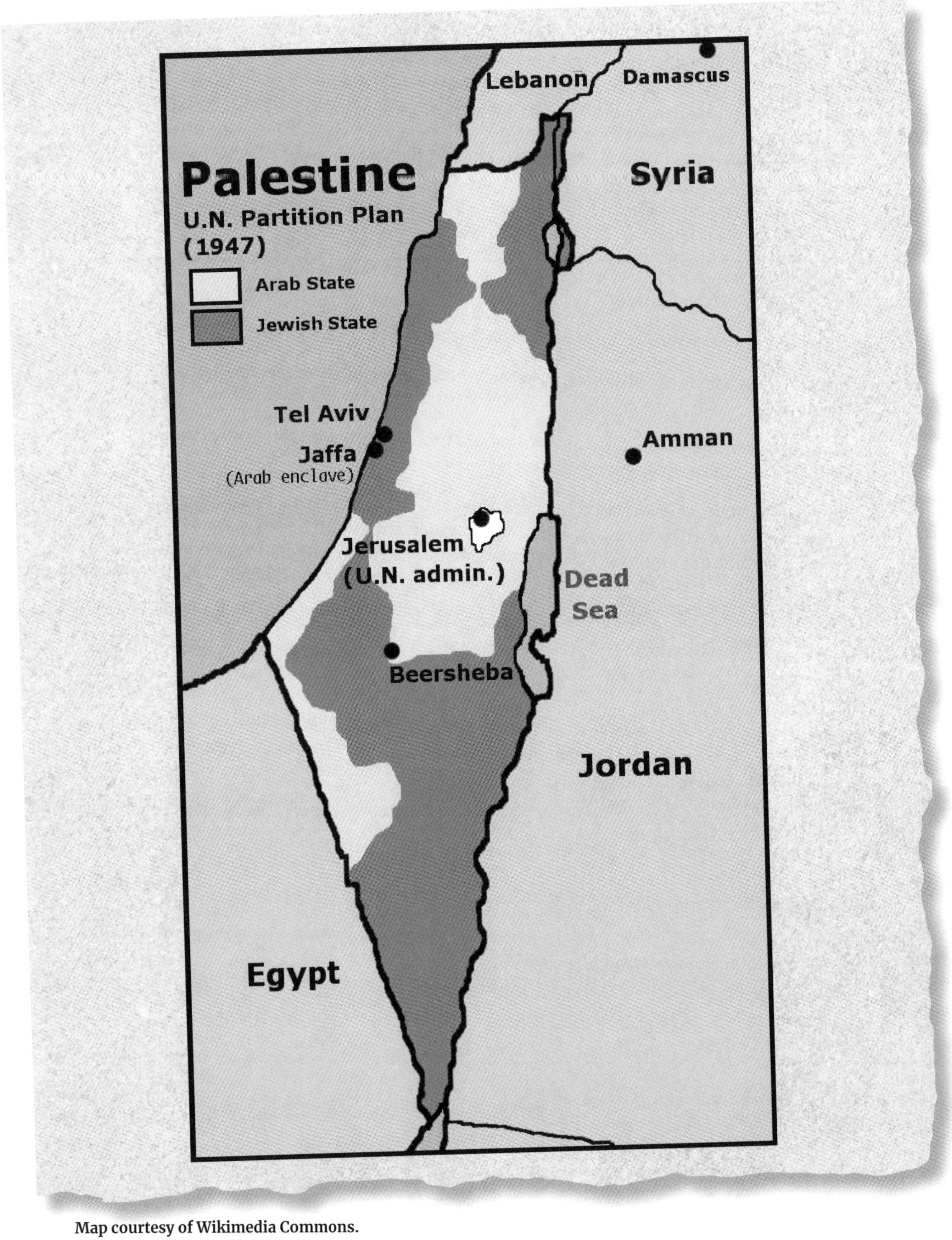

Map courtesy of Wikimedia Commons.

United Nations Resolution about Territories (1967)

SECURITY COUNCIL

Resolution 242 (1967) of 22 November 1967

22 November 1967

The Security Council,

Expressing its continuing concern with the grave situation in the Middle East,

Emphasizing the inadmissibility of the acquisition of territory by war and the need to work for a just and lasting peace in which every State in the area can live in security,

Emphasizing further that all Member States in their acceptance of the Charter of the United Nations have undertaken a commitment to act in accordance with Article 2 of the Charter,

1 *Affirms* that the fulfilment of Charter principles requires· the establishment of a just and lasting peace in the Middle East which should include the application of both the following principles:

(i) Withdrawal of Israel armed forces from <u>territories</u> occupied in the recent conflict;

(ii) Termination of all claims or states of belligerency and respect for and acknowledgment of the sovereignty, territorial integrity and political independence of every State in the area and their right to live in peace within secure and recognized boundaries free from threats or acts of force;

2 *Affirms further* the necessity

(a) For guaranteeing freedom of navigation through international waterways in the area;

(b) For achieving a just settlement of the refugee problem;

(c) For guaranteeing the territorial inviolability and political independence of every State in the area, through measures including the establishment of demilitarized zones;

3 *Requests* the Secretary-General to designate a Special Representative to proceed to the Middle East to establish and maintain contacts with the States concerned in order to promote agreement and assist efforts to achieve a peaceful and accepted settlement in accordance with the provisions and principles in this resolution;

4 *Requests* the Secretary-General to report to the Security Council on the progress of the efforts of the Special Representative as soon as possible.

Source: United Nations, www.un.org/unispal

Palestine National Charter, 1968

The Palestinian Liberation Organization (PLO) was founded in 1964. Its original covenant was amended in 1968 by the Palestine National Council.

Resolutions of the Palestine National Council July 1-17, 1968

Article 1: Palestine is the homeland of the Arab Palestinian people; it is an indivisible part of the Arab homeland, and the Palestinian people are an integral part of the Arab nation.

Article 2: Palestine, with the boundaries it had during the British Mandate, is an indivisible territorial unit.

Article 3: The Palestinian Arab people possess the legal right to their homeland and have the right to determine their destiny after achieving the liberation of their country in accordance with their wishes and entirely of their own accord and will.

Article 4: The Palestinian identity is a genuine, essential, and inherent characteristic; it is transmitted from parents to children. The Zionist occupation and the dispersal of the Palestinian Arab people, through the disasters which befell them, do not make them lose their Palestinian identity and their membership in the Palestinian community, nor do they negate them.

Article 5: The Palestinians are those Arab nationals who, until 1947, normally resided in Palestine regardless of whether they were evicted from it or have stayed there. Anyone born, after that date, of a Palestinian father—whether inside Palestine or outside it—is also a Palestinian.

Article 6: The Jews who had normally resided in Palestine until the beginning of the Zionist invasion will be considered Palestinians.

Article 7: That there is a Palestinian community and that it has material, spiritual, and historical connection with Palestine are indisputable facts. It is a national duty to bring up individual Palestinians in an Arab revolutionary manner. All means of information and education must be adopted in order to acquaint the Palestinian with his country in the most profound manner, both spiritual and material, that is possible. He must be prepared for the armed struggle and ready to sacrifice his wealth and his life in order to win back his homeland and bring about its liberation.

Article 8: The phase in their history, through which the Palestinian people are now living, is that of national (*watani*) struggle for the liberation of Palestine. Thus the conflicts among the Palestinian national forces are secondary, and should be ended for the sake of the basic conflict that exists between the forces of Zionism and of imperialism on the one hand, and the Palestinian Arab people on the other. On this basis the Palestinian masses, regardless of whether they are residing in the national homeland or in diaspora (*mahajir*) constitute—both their organizations and the individuals—one national front working for the retrieval of Palestine and its liberation through armed struggle.

Article 9: Armed struggle is the only way to liberate Palestine. This it is the overall strategy, not merely a tactical phase. The Palestinian Arab people assert their absolute determination and firm resolution to continue their armed struggle and to work for an armed popular revolution for the liberation of their country and their return to it. They also assert their right to normal life in Palestine and to exercise their right to self-determination and sovereignty over it.

Article 10: Commando action constitutes the nucleus of the Palestinian popular liberation war. This requires its escalation, comprehensiveness, and the mobilization of all the Palestinian popular and educational efforts and their organization and involvement in the armed Palestinian revolution. It also requires the achieving of unity for the national (*watani*) struggle among the different groupings of the Palestinian people, and between the Palestinian people and the Arab masses, so as to secure the continuation of the revolution, its escalation, and victory.

Article 11: The Palestinians will have three mottoes: national (*wataniyya*) unity, national (*qawmiyya*) mobilization, and liberation.

Article 12: The Palestinian people believe in Arab unity. In order to contribute their share toward the attainment of that objective, however, they must, at the present stage of their struggle, safeguard their Palestinian identity and develop their consciousness of that identity, and oppose any plan that may dissolve or impair it.

Article 13: Arab unity and the liberation of Palestine are two complementary objectives, the attainment of either of which facilitates the attainment of the other. Thus, Arab unity leads to the liberation of Palestine, the liberation of Palestine leads to Arab unity; and work toward the realization of one objective proceeds side by side with work toward the realization of the other.

Article 14: The destiny of the Arab nation, and indeed Arab existence itself, depend upon the destiny of the Palestine cause. From this interdependence springs the Arab nation's pursuit of, and striving for, the liberation of Palestine. The people of Palestine play the role of the vanguard in the realization of this sacred (*qawmi*) goal.

Article 15: The liberation of Palestine, from an Arab viewpoint, is a national (*qawmi*) duty and it attempts to repel the Zionist and imperialist aggression against the Arab homeland, and aims at the elimination of Zionism in Palestine. Absolute responsibility for this falls upon the Arab nation—peoples and governments—with the Arab people of Palestine in the vanguard. Accordingly, the Arab nation must mobilize all its military, human, moral, and spiritual capabilities to participate actively with the Palestinian people in the liberation of Palestine. It must, particularly in the phase of the armed Palestinian revolution, offer and furnish the Palestinian people with all possible help, and material and human support, and make available to them the means and opportunities that will enable them to continue to carry out their leading role in the armed revolution, until they liberate their homeland.

Article 16: The liberation of Palestine, from a spiritual point of view, will provide the Holy Land with an atmosphere of safety and tranquility, which in turn will safeguard the country's religious sanctuaries and guarantee freedom of worship and of visit to all, without discrimination of race, color, language, or religion. Accordingly, the people of Palestine look to all spiritual forces in the world for support.

Article 17: The liberation of Palestine, from a human point of view, will restore to the Palestinian individual his dignity, pride, and freedom. Accordingly the Palestinian Arab people look forward to the support of all those who believe in the dignity of man and his freedom in the world.

Article 18: The liberation of Palestine, from an international point of view, is a defensive action necessitated by the demands of self-defense. Accordingly the Palestinian people, desirous as they are of the friendship of all people, look to freedom-loving, and peace-loving states for support in order to restore their legitimate rights in Palestine, to re-establish peace and security in the country, and to enable its people to exercise national sovereignty and freedom.

Article 19: The partition of Palestine in 1947 and the establishment of the state of Israel are entirely illegal, regardless of the passage of time, because they were contrary to the will of the Palestinian people and to their natural right in their homeland, and inconsistent with the principles embodied in the Charter of the United Nations; particularly the right to self-determination.

Article 20: The Balfour Declaration, the Mandate for Palestine, and everything that has been based upon them, are deemed null and void. Claims of historical or religious ties of Jews with Palestine are incompatible with the facts of history and the true conception of what constitutes statehood. Judaism, being a religion, is not an independent nationality. Nor do Jews constitute a single nation with an identity of its own; they are citizens of the states to which they belong.

Article 21: The Arab Palestinian people, expressing themselves by the armed Palestinian revolution, reject all solutions which are substitutes for the total liberation of Palestine and reject all proposals aiming at the liquidation of the Palestinian problem, or its internationalization.

Palestine National Charter, 1968 (continued)

Article 22: Zionism is a political movement organically associated with international imperialism and antagonistic to all action for liberation and to progressive movements in the world. It is racist and fanatic in its nature, aggressive, expansionist, and colonial in its aims, and fascist in its methods. Israel is the instrument of the Zionist movement, and geographical base for world imperialism placed strategically in the midst of the Arab homeland to combat the hopes of the Arab nation for liberation, unity, and progress. Israel is a constant source of threat vis-a-vis peace in the Middle East and the whole world. Since the liberation of Palestine will destroy the Zionist and imperialist presence and will contribute to the establishment of peace in the Middle East, the Palestinian people look for the support of all the progressive and peaceful forces and urge them all, irrespective of their affiliations and beliefs, to offer the Palestinian people all aid and support in their just struggle for the liberation of their homeland.

Article 23: The demand of security and peace, as well as the demand of right and justice, require all states to consider Zionism an illegitimate movement, to outlaw its existence, and to ban its operations, in order that friendly relations among peoples may be preserved, and the loyalty of citizens to their respective homelands safeguarded.

Article 24: The Palestinian people believe in the principles of justice, freedom, sovereignty, self-determination, human dignity, and in the right of all peoples to exercise them.

Article 25: For the realization of the goals of this Charter and its principles, the Palestine Liberation Organization will perform its role in the liberation of Palestine in accordance with the Constitution of this Organization.

Article 26: The Palestine Liberation Organization, representative of the Palestinian revolutionary forces, is responsible for the Palestinian Arab people's movement in its struggle—to retrieve its homeland, liberate and return to it and exercise the right to self-determination in it—in all military, political, and financial fields and also for whatever may be required by the Palestine case on the inter-Arab and international levels.

Article 27: The Palestine Liberation Organization shall cooperate with all Arab states, each according to its potentialities; and will adopt a neutral policy among them in the light of the requirements of the war of liberation; and on this basis it shall not interfere in the internal affairs of any Arab state.

Article 28: The Palestinian Arab people assert the genuineness and independence of their national (*wataniyya*) revolution and reject all forms of intervention, trusteeship, and subordination.

Article 29: The Palestinian people possess the fundamental and genuine legal right to liberate and retrieve their homeland. The Palestinian people determine their attitude toward all states and forces on the basis of the stands they adopt vis-a-vis to the Palestinian revolution to fulfill the aims of the Palestinian people.

Article 30: Fighters and carriers of arms in the war of liberation are the nucleus of the popular army which will be the protective force for the gains of the Palestinian Arab people.

Article 31: The Organization shall have a flag, an oath of allegiance, and an anthem. All this shall be decided upon in accordance with a special regulation.

Article 32: Regulations, which shall be known as the Constitution of the Palestinian Liberation Organization, shall be annexed to this Charter. It will lay down the manner in which the Organization, and its organs and institutions, shall be constituted; the respective competence of each; and the requirements of its obligation under the Charter.

Article 33: This Charter shall not be amended save by [vote of] a majority of two-thirds of the total membership of the National Congress of the Palestine Liberation Organization [taken] at a special session convened for that purpose.

Source: Center for Israel Education; The Avalon Project of Yale Law School

Camp David Accords, Explained

Camp David Accords: Egyptian-Israeli History

By Jimmy Carter

Camp David Accords were agreements between Israel and Egypt signed on September 17, 1978, that led to a peace treaty between those two countries, the first such treaty between Israel and any of its Arab neighbours. Brokered by U.S. President Jimmy Carter between Israeli Prime Minister Menachem Begin and Egyptian President Anwar el-Sādāt and officially titled the "Framework for Peace in the Middle East," the agreements became known as the Camp David Accords because the negotiations took place at the U.S. presidential retreat at Camp David in Maryland. Sādāt and Begin were awarded the Nobel Prize for Peace in 1978 for their contributions to the agreements.

Background

The United Nations (UN) voted in 1947 to partition Great Britain's Palestine mandate—to be established were a Jewish state, an Arab state, and an independent Jerusalem under a UN trusteeship. Arabs opposed partition. When the mandate ended on May 15, 1948, and Israel proclaimed its independence, the first Arab-Israeli war erupted. No separate state for Arab Palestinians (i.e., Palestinians) was established. Egypt took control of the Gaza Strip along the Mediterranean Sea, and Jordan assumed sovereignty over the territory between Israel's eastern border and the Jordan River (the West Bank), including East Jerusalem. During the Six-Day War of June 1967, Israel occupied those territories as well as the Golan Heights—a patch of Syrian land on Israel's northeastern border—and Egypt's Sinai Peninsula. Following his election as U.S. president, Carter committed himself to working toward a comprehensive Middle East peace settlement based on UN Resolution 242 (November 1967), which called for the withdrawal of Israel from the occupied territories, Arab recognition of and peace with Israel (stipulations that the Arab states had refused to agree to), and a just settlement to the problem of Palestinian refugees displaced by the establishment of Israel and the 1967 war.

In November 1977, Sādāt initiated direct contacts with Israel and made a dramatic visit to Jerusalem, where he spoke to the Israeli Knesset. However, a reciprocal visit by Begin was unsuccessful, and no progress was made toward peace. Rosalynn Carter, the U.S. first lady, then suggested to her husband that he invite Sādāt and Begin to Camp David, in rural Maryland, where the relative privacy and seclusion might provide a setting for a breakthrough.

The Summit

The two leaders accepted Carter's invitation, and the summit began on September 5, 1978, and lasted for 13 days. It was extremely unusual for heads of state to engage in a summit meeting at which the outcome was so much in doubt. Not only had Egypt and Israel been at war for decades, but the personality differences of the leaders promised to complicate the dialogue. Begin, always formal in dress and manner, was extremely detail-oriented and careful about the possible ramifications of any agreements. He was pessimistic about what he believed could be achieved at Camp David and insisted that the objective be limited to developing an agenda for future meetings. By contrast, Sādāt wore fashionable sports clothes, was relaxed and forthcoming, and was willing to join in comprehensive negotiations aimed at settling all controversial issues during the few days of the summit.

All three men were accompanied by their leading foreign policy advisers, but Carter preferred that the three men work together in private sessions in a small office at Aspen, his cabin at Camp David. He also insisted that there be no direct press coverage of the meetings, fearing it would have a negative

Camp David Accords, Explained (continued)

effect on negotiations. A humorous situation arose right before the first meeting, an awkward moment that nonetheless shed light on the personalities involved. After President Carter and the first lady entered the cabin, Begin and Sādāt hesitated over who should follow through the doorway. Both men laughed, and Begin insisted that Sādāt proceed first. As the first lady noted later, "Jimmy said to me that Begin would never go ahead of Sādāt, being perfectly proper according to protocol—president above prime minister."

After three days of negotiations, the heated discussions reached an impasse, and direct discourse between Sādāt and Begin became impossible. Carter then compiled a single document that encompassed a resolution of the major issues, presented the proposals to each leader in separate meetings, assessed their comments, and redrafted the manuscript some two dozen times, shuttling the manuscript back and forth for their review.

As the days passed, prospects for a settlement at Camp David appeared so bleak that Sādāt threatened to leave, and Carter began planning to return to the White House and suffer the likely political consequences of failure. An agreement was reached on the final day.

A Framework For Peace

The eventual outcome of these talks, the "Framework for Peace in the Middle East," had three parts: (1) a process for Palestinian self-government in the West Bank and Gaza, (2) a framework for the conclusion of a peace treaty between Egypt and Israel, and (3) a similar framework for peace treaties between Israel and its other neighbours. The prime minister and the Israeli Knesset agreed that a transitional self-governing Palestinian authority was to be elected to replace Israeli political and military forces in the occupied territories.

The peace treaty that Israel and Egypt signed in March 1979. Israel agreed to withdraw from Sinai, and Egypt promised to establish normal diplomatic relations between the two countries and open the Suez Canal to Israeli ships (which until then had been banned from the waterway). These provisions were duly carried out. However, most Arab countries, rather than following Egypt's lead, ostracized Egypt and expelled it from the Arab League. The Palestine Liberation Organization (PLO), professing to speak for the Palestinian people, also rejected the accords. Nonetheless, the next major advance in Middle East peace negotiations, the Oslo Accords signed by Israel and the PLO in 1993, included provisions with regard to the West Bank and Gaza that were similar to those in the Camp David Accords.

How to Communicate in Conflict

Encounter is an organization that focuses on forging relationships between American Jewish leaders and Palestinians so they can be a positive force for communal change around the subject of the Israeli-Palestinian conflict.

Encounter's approach to communicating in conflict aims to create a framework in which deeply contentious and charged topics can be explored respectfully by people of diverse ideological viewpoints.

This approach helps us:

- hear and learn things we might otherwise miss, and
- ask challenging questions in ways that can be heard by the person being addressed.

While it may feel counterintuitive at first, using this framework can actually liberate us. First, we are forced to clarify for ourselves and for others the burning question at the heart of our discomfort or curiosity; second, we are able to communicate more openly because we are no longer afraid of offending. Encounter's approach enables us to ask the most challenging questions in ways that are respectful, genuine, and open.

Encounter's approach to communicating in conflict enables us to speak with כבוד / kavod (honor) and אמת emet (truthfulness) in all our conversations. It serves as a guiding framework for conversations with other participants as well as with Palestinians.

We encourage participants to:

1. **Speak for yourself, not as a representative of a group.** Do not ask others to represent, defend or explain an entire group. Make "I" statements rather than "we" statements.
2. **Avoid making broad generalizations and grand pronouncements.** Instead, connect what you know and believe to your experiences and sources of information.
3. **Express your different viewpoints in a thoughtful manner** and without an insulting spirit. Keep in mind your goals of learning and reflection. When you disagree with others, respectfully express your opinions, but resist the urge to persuade them to "your side."
4. **Listen with resilience**, "hanging in" when you hear something that is hard to hear. Take personal time if you find that you are no longer able to listen with a clear mind and an open heart.
5. **Share airtime and refrain from interrupting others**, except to indicate that you cannot hear a speaker. Participate within the time frames suggested by the facilitators.
6. **"Pass" or "pass for now"** if you are not ready or willing to respond to a question, no explanation required.
7. **Keep all small-group conversations and listening pairs confidential.** Outside those, if asked to keep something confidential, honor the request. In conversations outside of the group, do not attribute statements to individuals by name or identifying information without permission.
8. During question and answer time periods, **avoid making lengthy statements.** Do not argue with speakers or other participants. Instead, ask questions that express your genuine curiosity.

Settlements, Peace, and Security Source Sheet

1

And I will give to you and your children after you the land of your sojournings, the entire land of Canaan, for an everlasting holding. I will be their God.

(Genesis 17:8)

2

Hillel says: "Be among the disciples of Aaron, loving peace and pursuing peace...."

(Pirkei Avot 1:12)

3

One of the biggest problems that all Palestinians complain about is the lack of a clear future. Over the past 20 years, we have lived through periods of hope, violence, anticipation, concern....We do not know what the future holds for us. Every single event that happens on the political side can flip all your plans.

(Nedal Zahran, Palestinian on the West Bank)

4

Living here is a major part of our patriotism. By building our homes and raising our children here, we are reviving the historical connection of our people with our land. That is what Zionism is all about.

(David Ha'ivri, Israeli settler, Kfar Tapuach, West Bank)

5

From the Palestinian village of Tuwani

For their protection, Keifa Jundiyye and other Palestinian children are escorted to school each day by international volunteers and Israeli soldiers. In the past, rock- throwing Jewish settlers have thrown rocks at students. In some cases, families have chosen to no longer send their children to school in order to avoid injury. "Education is a mighty weapon. It is the only weapon we have," says Jundiyye.

6

From the Jewish settlement of Amona

Yair (18) used text messaging to organize teens to protest against the government's evacuation of Amona, his settlement. The Israeli government considered Amona illegal and had struck a deal with the settlement's elders to close Amona and resettle its residents. But when soldiers came to evacuate Amona, the teenagers refused to leave and barricaded themselves in buildings. Most of the teens eventually left peacefully, but some threw rocks, paint, and bleach at the military. "I think the fight for Amona is not finished," said Yair, and explained that he felt it was important that the world know that Jews were being uprooted from land that he believes God had granted them.

7

From the Israeli town of S'derot, near Gaza (not in the West Bank)

Carmit Malka and her husband, Oshri were born and raised in S'derot, and now raise their sons, Noam (age 6) and Idan (age 4), there.

The family had left just a half-hour earlier to take the children to school and head to work when a rocket launched from the nearby Gaza Strip destroyed their home.

"I remember growing up, feeling safe and secure in S'derot. I was happy. Why can't my kids have that kind of childhood?" Carmit wonders.

Chapter 7 It's a Part of the World Community

Words to Know:

ambassador: a government-appointed representative of one country to another country

BDS movement: a group highly critical of Israel and its policies that works to convince governments and individuals to boycott Israeli products, divest from Israeli companies, and sanction Israel with punishing laws

Buy Israel: a movement to counter the work of BDS by encouraging people to support Israeli companies by buying Israeli products

J Street: a Jewish American organization whose goal is to promote peace in Israel through a two-state solution; it often disagrees with Israel's policies

Introduction

Enduring Understanding:

Israel's unique position on the world stage means it has positive relationships with some countries and negative relationships with other countries.

Chapter Overview:

This chapter highlights some of the economic and cultural partnerships and political ties between Israel and other countries, and the humanitarian work Israel has done around the world. It also explores the harsh judgments—some deserved, some not—Israel receives from other countries, the media, and protest groups. It asks students to consider whether it is okay to criticize Israel and, if so, under what circumstances.

Chapter 7 Lesson 1

Positive and Negative Relationships with Israel

Essential Question: Why does Israel have strong relationships with some countries and face harsh criticism and even threats from others?

Learning Objectives: Students will be able to:

- Articulate some of the ways in which Israel has built strong relationships and partnerships with other nations.
- Understand that Israel is sometimes criticized by other countries and organizations.
- Explore the way media bias can sometimes play into the way Israel is perceived.

Materials:

- markers
- poster board (optional)
- Conan O'Brien videos at bhlink.me/israel7
- *Values in Action* video at bhlink.me/israel7
- copies of news articles or blog posts about Israel, found on pages 136–138 of this guide, at bhlink.me/israel7, or your own examples

Activities

Getting Started (10 minutes)

Working individually or with partners, ask students to choose an issue that affects people in their community, state, or country (such as homelessness, hunger, protecting the environment, or animal rights) that they feel needs more attention. Distribute blank paper and markers for students to make a sign they could carry on a march to encourage the support of others for this important issue. Help them hang their completed signs around the room. Give students a few minutes to look at their classmates' work and ask:

What do the posters tell you about your community? What do the posters tell you about each other? *(The posters identify problems that our neighbors may be facing; the posters may show inequality—some people have a lot, while others are homeless or hungry. The posters show that our community cares about important issues, and that we work hard to address problems and help people in need.)*

Building Activity: With One Voice

If all or most of the students in the class are passionate about one particular issue, speak to your education director about staging an actual rally in support of that cause in your classroom, in the hallway, or even in front of your school. Ask students to make signs on poster board that they could hold up and carry. Be sure to videotape the rally.

What Do You See? (5 minutes)

Say to students:

Around the world, some people celebrate Israel, while others protest it. With a partner, look at the pictures at the bottom of page 72 and answer the questions. Then we'll discuss them as a group.

1 How does it feel to see that some of the people protesting are Jewish? *(Students might be surprised to learn that Jews are protesting against Israel. Some students might appreciate that their fellow Jews are advocating for Israel.)*

2 If you could speak with one of the protestors or with one of Israel's supporters, what would you want to ask? What would you want to say? (*Protestors: Students might want to ask why they are upset with Israel, or why they feel the need to speak up against Israel. They might agree or disagree with their decision to protest, so they may wish to thank them for their protest or explain why they believe Jews shouldn't protest against Israel. Supporters: Students might want to thank them for speaking up on behalf of Israel, or they might want to know if they have any criticisms of Israel.)*

3 These kinds of images are shared in the media around the world. How do you think seeing them affects people's opinions of Israel? *(All of the protest pictures may cause people to have a negative perception of Israel and Israelis; this might be heightened by seeing that Jews are some of the people protesting. Seeing people supporting Israel might help people understand how important Israel is to so many Jews around the world.)*

Conan O'Brien (10 minutes)

Say to students:

In 2017, comedian Conan O'Brien visited Israel and created videos that depicted his trip. Let's watch some videos (bhlink.me/israel7), then I'd like you each to pick one and write a short review of it on page 73 of your books.

When students have completed their reviews, ask:

Why is it important for people to see this side of Israel? How can influential people, like Conan O'Brien, help to raise awareness? *(Since so much media coverage of Israel focuses on the conflicts in the region, it is important for people to see that Israelis are also just regular people, with a sense of humor, living their lives.).*

Values in Action (10 minutes)

Invite one or two volunteers to read "Lifesaving around the World" on page 74, then show the video at bhlink.me/israel7 about the work of Israeli organizations such as the IDF Medical Corps. With partners, ask students to answer the questions at the bottom of the page.

1 What values do you think inspire Israelis to do this work and the work shown in the photos above? *(Israelis are often guided by Jewish values. For example, the value of piku'ach nefesh, "saving a life," is a strong motivational force in much of the humanitarian work Israel does. Israelis also believe in protecting and helping people in times of need, treating others with respect and kindness, and working toward tikun olam, "repairing the world.")*

2 In what ways do you think these experiences affect relationships between Israelis and people around the world? *(For many people, this is their first direct contact with Israelis. It helps them to see that many Israelis are kind, compassionate people who are working toward making the world a better place. It helps counteract some of the negative coverage Israel receives in the media and from other organizations around the world.)*

3 In what ways did watching the video and seeing these photos affect your own feelings about Israel? *(I was inspired by the incredibly meaningful work Israelis are doing to help people in need around the world. It was interesting to learn that Israelis even help people from countries that are currently in conflict with Israel. I wish more people knew about this side of Israel.)*

Headlines and Israel (10 minutes)

Spread out on one table copies of news articles or blog posts that are critical of Israel. On another table, spread out copies of news articles or blog posts favorable to Israel. You can use the stories on pages 136–138 of this guide or at bhlink.me/israel7, or bring in stories that you have found. Have students work with partner and read one of the critical stories and answer the following questions:

1 How does it feel to see Israel criticized in the news? *(It makes me sad to see a place I care about being treated this way. It makes me feel like I need to defend Israel. I'm not sure; I have some of the same criticisms, but I don't like seeing other people making them. It inspires me to want to raise awareness about Israel.)*

2 What criticisms does the post or article make against Israel? Write these on page 75 of your books, leaving room for answers to question 4, or on separate paper. (*The answers to questions 2 through 5 will depend on specifics of the post or article.)*

3 Do you think the criticism is fair or unfair? Why?

Now, ask students to choose one of the positive articles about Israel. Say:

4 Write its main points in your books or on a separate paper.

5 Do you think the positive descriptions in the article are fair or unfair? Why?

End this lesson on a positive note by asking students, working with their partners or in small groups, to write a positive article or blog post about an Israeli organization like IDF Medical Corps or Israel Flying Aid. When they are done, ask students to share their work with the class.

Chapter 7 Lesson 2

Supporting Israel, Criticizing Israel

Essential Question: How can we both support Israel and offer criticism of Israel when we feel it is appropriate?

Learning Objectives: Students will be able to:

- Explain that there are some individuals and groups that are critical of Israel and its policies.
- Identify positive relationships that individuals and groups have with Israel.
- Understand differing perspectives on whether and how it is appropriate to criticize Israel.

Materials:

- tablets/smartphones to record and play videos (optional)

Activities

Getting Started (15 minutes)

After reading pages 76 and 77 (or asking for volunteers to read), invite three students to each read aloud one of the quotes by Roger Waters, J. K. Rowling, or Mahmoud Abbas. Working with a friend, ask them to discuss the following questions:

1. How would you feel if a band or actor you liked decided to boycott Israel? Would you still be a fan? *(Students might decide to no longer attend the band's concerts or see movies in which the actor has a role. They might also decide that perspectives on Israel won't shape their interest in performers' music or movies.)*
2. How do you feel about J. K. Rowling's point that cultural boycotts are being proposed against Israel and not against countries like North Korea and Zimbabwe? *(When countries with serious human rights violations are being ignored while Israel is being singled out, it is important to question what other issues are in play; many believe that the underlying difference is anti-Semitism.)*
3. Were you surprised to see the president of the Palestinian Authority speaking out against boycotts of Israel? Why do you think he feels that way? *(Many Palestinians are dependent on the Israeli economy for their livelihoods. The boycotts may hurt the people he is representing. Some feel that the boycotts may actually undermine efforts toward peace rather than encourage the peace process.)*

Building Activity: Opinions in the Family

This activity (page 77 in the student book), a video interview, is a way to include your students' families in a meaningful discussion about Israel. It would be helpful to send an email home to parents in advance, explaining the activity and sharing the questions. Here is a sample email:

Dear Parents,

We are learning about differing perspectives on Israel. Students are being asked to interview two adults in their lives, such as parents, grandparents, or family friends, about their views on Israel. Students can document the interview in writing, then film a short video on a smartphone or tablet. Students will be asked to share their interviews in class when we next meet.

Interview Questions:

- How would you describe your relationship with the State of Israel? With its people?
- What's your favorite thing about Israel?
- What concerns do you have about Israel?
- Do you disagree with any of Israel's policies?
- How do you feel about criticizing Israel?

Teacher Tip: If you have a class website, you may wish to ask families to upload the interviews there. Or families can share the videos with you via Google Drive or send in a thumb drive so you can view them as a class.

After students have shared their completed interviews/videos with a partner or viewed them as a class, ask them to discuss the following four questions:

1. Were any of the answers surprising to you?
2. Which opinions matched your own views? Were there any with which you disagreed?
3. In what ways did the interviewees agree with one another? Disagree?
4. How did hearing different opinions on the same topic impact your own views?

Building Activity: Two Jews, Three Opinions

Work with your education director, principal, or rabbi to invite community members with a range of perspectives on Israel to visit your class. Give students a chance to ask them the bulleted questions at the top of page 77 and questions of their own.

Debate It: Can We Criticize Israel? (20 minutes)

Invite volunteers to read "Can We Criticize Israel?" on page 78 of the student book and the "Debate It" directions at the top of page 79. Remind students that it is important to be respectful of people with opinions different from their own. After partners have discussed whether it is okay to write an article critical of Israel for their school newspaper and listed the main points of their debate, ask volunteers to share their perspectives with the class:

YES! I can criticize Israel because: ________________________________

(To maintain a strong democracy, it is important to support a free press and the free expression of opinion in my country and in Israel. My family/synagogue/community contributes money to support projects in Israel; if we are asked to contribute financially, we have a right to express our opinions about Israeli policies. We all have a responsibility to speak out against injustice no matter where it occurs.)

NO! I shouldn't be critical of Israel because: ________________________________

(As a Jew, it makes me feel uncomfortable to criticize Israel. As a Jew, I take criticism of Israel personally. There are so many individuals/organizations/countries that express disapproval of Israel; I don't wish to add to the negativity. If Jews do not support Israel, others will not support Israel.)

Then, ask students to discuss a third possibility with their partners:

Maybe! It's sometimes okay to criticize Israel, but not always. When do you think it would be okay? When would it not be okay? ________________________________

(This will depend on students' personal views.)

Reflection: Talk about It! (10 minutes)

In small groups ask students to discuss the questions at the bottom of page 79. Then, ask representatives from each group to share their group's answers with the class.

- In what ways did your own opinions about Israel change after you heard the stories in this chapter? *(Students may have felt more defensive about Israel after learning about the groups that are criticizing and boycotting it. They might be proud of the humanitarian work that Israel is doing around the world. They might have a deeper understanding of how media bias impacts the perceptions others have of Israel.)*
- If you were going to work to support Israel, in what way would you choose to do so? *(By writing letters to the editor refuting negative stories on Israel, by speaking up against anti-Zionist groups on my school campus, by raising money for Israeli organizations doing charitable work, by purchasing Israeli products, etc.)*
- If you were going to criticize Israel, how would you choose to do so? *(By protesting events I view as unethical, by engaging in dialogue with kids who have different opinions on Israel, by sending letters to the Israeli embassy in my own country, by spending time researching issues to ensure I have all the facts before offering criticism.)*

Additional Resources

The following activities and information can supplement the lessons or be used on their own to enrich learning about Israel as part of the world community.

Israel Brings Eye Care to Africa

How Hadassah Revolutionized Eye Care in Africa

Hadassah Magazine, August 2018

By Wendy Elliman

In 1959, Liberian President William Tubman broke his glasses. As Liberia had no opticians, optometrists or ophthalmologists, his choice was waiting three weeks for glasses to come from London, or going there to get them. Then a third option emerged: Ask Israel for help.

His request reached Dr. Isaac Michaelson, then head of Hadassah's Department of Ophthalmology. Dr. Michaelson went to Liberia, examined the president's eyes and those of his family, and helped Tubman get a new pair of glasses. At the invitation of the president, Dr. Michaelson surveyed eye care throughout the nation. Within a year, that survey resulted in a 30-bed ophthalmic hospital in Liberia's capital, Monrovia, run by six Hadassah physicians, while seven Liberian doctors and nurses trained at Hadassah.

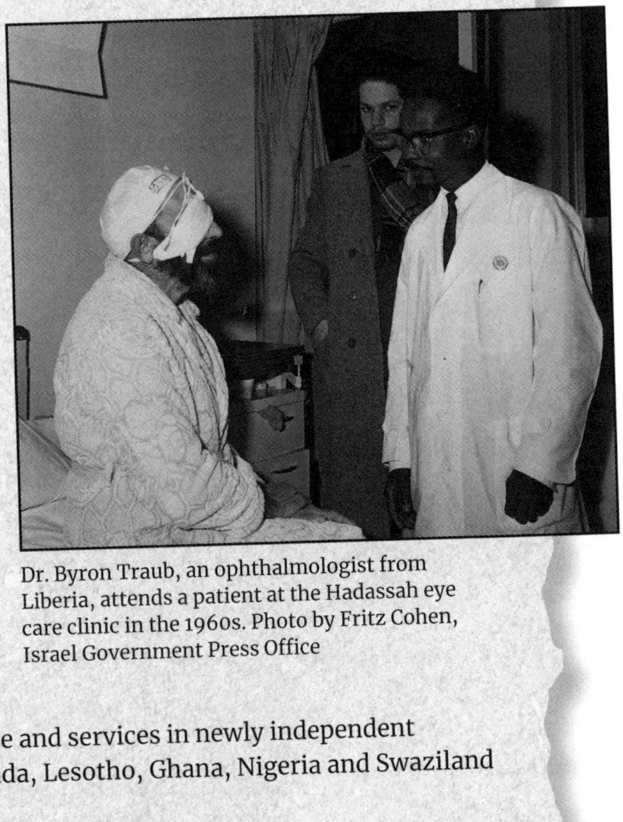

Dr. Byron Traub, an ophthalmologist from Liberia, attends a patient at the Hadassah eye care clinic in the 1960s. Photo by Fritz Cohen, Israel Government Press Office

That was just the beginning of Hadassah's outreach to Africa. During the 1960s, Hadassah reviewed eye disease and services in newly independent Botswana, Tanzania, Ivory Coast, Ethiopia, Malawi, Rwanda, Lesotho, Ghana, Nigeria and Swaziland and helped those nations set up eye clinics and hospitals.

Dr. Michaelson made acceptance to Hadassah's senior ophthalmic residency program conditional on a minimum two-year service in Africa—resulting in a total of 48 Hadassah ophthalmologists helping establish modern eye care in Africa. (With African ophthalmology now largely self-sufficient, Hadassah's help today takes the form of two- to four-week missions to treat patients and guide doctors.)

Israel Bring Eye Care to Africa (continued)

By the early 1970s, Israeli-trained African doctors were heading medical departments and Health Ministry divisions in a dozen African nations. At the June ophthalmology conference in Jerusalem, Dr. Hugh Taylor of Melbourne, Australia, president of the International Council of Ophthalmology, recalled first encountering Hadassah in Liberia 40 years ago. "Every ophthalmologist I met there had trained at Hadassah!" he said. "A decade later, working in Kenya, I met a young Israeli physician named Jacob Pe'er, who was there setting up the entire ophthalmology department at Nakuru Provincial General Hospital. When I first visited Hadassah in Jerusalem two years ago, I was amazed that only a third of its ophthalmology trainees were Israeli. A third were Palestinian and the remainder international."

When the 1973 Yom Kippur War severed relations between Israel and much of Africa, then-Hadassah ophthalmology head Dr. Hanan Zauberman developed a five-year specialization program for qualified physicians from Latin America. The first candidates were from Ecuador, Peru, Panama and Mexico.

Today, the program has expanded and its graduates come from Africa, Latin America, Asia and Europe—as well as from the West Bank and Gaza. One of 15 foreign physicians and fellows currently studying in the program is Dr. Vofo Brite, a young ophthalmologist from Cameroon, in Central Africa. "My country's population is twice that of Israel, but we have only two retinal specialists," he told conference attendees. "My aim is to be the third."

"Some 126 ophthalmologists from 37 countries have done residencies and specializations at Hadassah," Dr. Jesus Vidaurri, a leading ophthalmic surgeon at Mexico's Centro de Oftalmología San José, shared. "I'm one of them. What I learned at Hadassah inspired me to change eye care in my community."

Source: Reprinted with permission from *Hadassah Magazine*

Israeli Technology Helps Cave-Trapped Thai Boys

Times of Israel

ISRAELI TECHNOLOGY PROVIDING VITAL COMMUNICATIONS LINK TO CAVE-TRAPPED THAI BOYS

Maxtech Networks system has linked a "daisy-chain" of radio devise through twisting, water-submerged cavern, giving youths' voice, data, and video connection to the outside world.

By STUART WINER
5 July 2018

Rescuers working to save a Thai youth soccer team trapped deep inside a flooded cave are using an Israeli technology to maintain communication with the 12 boys and their coach.

Maxtech Networks told The Times of Israel that its system is providing a voice, data, and video link to the boys who have been stuck in the cave for nearly two weeks, and were only located earlier this week.

The boys, aged 11 to 16, and their 25-year-old coach entered the sprawling Tham Luang Nang Non cave in the northern province of Chiang Rai after a soccer game on June 23. They were found by two British rescue divers on July 2, nine days after they disappeared.

In the Israeli system, a string of small devices, similar to handheld radios, pass wireless communications between each other, enabling a link in places regular radios won't work, such as where there are major obstacles blocking the line-of-sight between the two ends of the line.

"It is like a daisy-chain," explained Uzi Hanuni, CEO of Maxtech.

It took 19 of the devices to complete the link to the boys in the cave. They have enough battery power for 10 hours' use at a time.

"It is a very complex scenario inside the cave," Hanuni explained.

Some sections of the perilous, twisting, passageway, estimated to be over a kilometer in length, are also submerged beneath the rainwater floods that trapped the youths. Hanuni said that data cables were used to traverse those parts of the cave.

After an Israeli acquaintance who runs a rescue team in Thailand and was involved in the early efforts to find the boys contacted Hanuni, Maxtech employee Yuval Zalmanov flew out to Thailand on June 25, bringing the equipment with him in a suitcase.

"We are happy to be able to help," Hanuni said and added he expects an attempt to extract the children to be made in the coming days. Others have said it may take weeks or months till such an attempt would be made.

Authorities said the boys, who appeared skinny but in good health in several videos released by the Thai navy, were being looked after by seven members of the Thai SEALs, including medics, who were staying with them inside the cave. They were mostly in stable condition and have received high-protein drinks.

Officials have said they prefer to get the boys out as soon as possible because heavy rain is expected to start by Saturday, which almost surely will raise water levels again in the cave, making passage in some areas even more difficult if not impossible.

Following their success in Thailand, Hanuni said he now wants to set up a quick response team, equipped with their technology, which would be ready to travel to emergencies all over the world.

Source: Times of Israel

UN Resolution (1975): Zionism is Racism

After the end of Israel's 1948 Independence War, no treaties were signed between Arab states and Israel. Led by Egypt in the 1950s and 1960s, Arab states waged political war and economic boycott against Israel in order to denigrate it directly and through the United Nations. In supporting its Arab clients, the USSR stood strong in every effort to delegitimize Israel, particularly at the UN. Moscow instigated the passage of the resolution, with it receiving support from Arab and Muslim states, Communist Bloc countries, about half of the African states, and some Asian countries. The resolution passed, 72–35 with 32 abstentions. The resolution "determines that Zionism is a form of racism and racial discrimination." Israel's Ambassador to the UN, Chaim Herzog rose in defense of Israel, pointing out Israel's inclusiveness with its Arab population, and labelled the resolution bitterly anti-Semitic, reflective of "anti-Jewish hatred which animates Arab society." The Resolution was revoked in December 1991, but the effort to delegitimize Israel internationally continued in Muslim and Arab states, and elsewhere.

—Ken Stein, Center for Israel Education

Zionism is Racism UN General Assembly Resolution 3379

November 10, 1975

The General Assembly,

Recalling its resolution 1904 (XVIII) of 20 November 1963, proclaiming the United Nations Declaration on the Elimination of All Forms of Racial Discrimination, and in particular its affirmation that "any doctrine of racial differentiation or superiority is scientifically false, morally condemnable, socially unjust and dangerous" and its expression of alarm at "the manifestations of racial discrimination still in evidence in some areas in the world, some of which are imposed by certain Governments by means of legislative, administrative or other measures",

Recalling also that, in its resolution 3151 G (XXVIII) of 14 December 1973, the General Assembly condemned, *inter alia*, the unholy alliance between South African racism and Zionism,

Taking note of the Declaration of Mexico on the Equality of Women and Their Contribution to Development and Peace 1975, proclaimed by the World Conference of the International Women's Year, held at Mexico City from 19 June to 2 July 1975, which promulgated the principle that "international co-operation and peace require the achievement of national liberation and independence, the elimination of colonialism and neo-colonialism, foreign occupation, Zionism, *apartheid* and racial discrimination in all its forms, as well as the recognition of the dignity of peoples and their right to self-determination",

Taking note also of resolution 77 (XII) adopted by the Assembly of Heads of State and Government of the Organization of African Unity at its twelfth ordinary session, held at Kampala from 28 July to 1 August 1975, which considered "that the racist regime in occupied Palestine and the racist regime in Zimbabwe and South Africa have a common imperialist origin, forming a whole and having the same racist structure and being organically linked in their policy aimed at repression of the dignity and integrity of the human being",

Taking note also of the Political Declaration and Strategy to Strengthen International Peace and Security and to Intensify Solidarity and Mutual Assistance among Non-Aligned Countries, adopted at the Conference of Ministers for Foreign Affairs of Non-Aligned Countries held at Lima from 25 to 30 August 1975, which most severely condemned Zionism as a threat to world peace and security and called upon all countries to oppose this racist and imperialist ideology,

Determines that Zionism is a form of racism and racial discrimination.

Source: United Nations

UN Resolution (1991): Zionism is Not Racism

United Nations

A/RES/46/86

General Assembly

Distr. GENERAL

16 December 1991

ORIGINAL:
ENGLISH

A/RES/46/86
74th plenary meeting
16 December 1991

Elimination of racism and racial discrimination

The General Assembly

Decides to revoke the determination contained in its resolution 3379 (XXX) of 10 November 1975.

Source: United Nations

Criticizing Israel: A Debate Activity

By Aviva Werner

The debate over whether and how to criticize the State of Israel and its policies is a complicated one. In this lesson, students consider how they can identify with and support Israel and still disagree with some of its actions.

Essential Question:

Should we criticize policies of the State of Israel?

Objectives:

- Students will articulate their praises and their criticisms of Israel.
- Students will understand that it is not a contradiction to be committed to and critical of Israel at the same time.
- Students will create a graphic representation of their feelings about Israel.

Activities

1. Draw a line down the center of the board. As a class, brainstorm a list of things for which Israel should be praised. Write the list on the left side of the board.
2. Next, as a class, brainstorm a list of the class's criticisms of Israel, whether political or social in nature. Write this list on the right side of the board. Ask:
    - Does it make sense to be committed to something of which we are critical?
3. Give each student a piece of paper. Have them draw a line down the center of the page, as you did on the board. Ask each student to think of someone they care for—a friend or relative. Without writing down the person's name, students should compose a list of things for which the person should be praised on the left side of the paper (for example, he is a good cook, he helps me with my homework) and criticisms of the person on the right side of the paper (for example, he has an annoying habit, he is sometimes forgetful). After a few minutes of quiet writing, discuss:
    - Does it make sense to care for this person of whom you are sometimes critical?
    - How can your criticisms of the person be an expression of friendship or affection?
    - Likewise, how can our criticisms of Israel be an expression of our support for Israel?

- How might your criticisms of the person be different if you disliked him or her rather than cared for him or her?

Watch the video, "Jon Stewart Learns What Happens When You Talk about Israel," available at bhlink.me/Israel7. Ask:

- Obviously this is meant to be funny. What point is the video making through its humor?
- What do you expect is the American Jewish community's reaction when someone pro-Palestinian criticizes Israel?
- What do you expect is the American Jewish community's reaction when someone pro-Israel criticizes Israel?
- What reaction would we get if we aired our class's criticisms of Israel in public?

4 Read the article "Criticizing Israel" as a class. Discuss:

- How do you think Burnat feels toward Israel? What do you think he said at his speaking engagement at Binghamton University?
- What do you think Burnat is trying to accomplish by encouraging boycotts, divestment, and sanctions against Israel?
- What do you think about Sheridan's decision to invite Burnat to speak?
- What do you think of the Hillel's reaction, asking Sheridan to step down from the Hillel board?
- How would you want to engage in dialogue with someone who is trying to damage Israel?
- Does everyone deserve to have a voice in a political dialogue? Should a terrorist or murderer be given a podium? Please discuss your answer.

5 Sum up the discussion: Do we Jews outside of Israel, who are mostly removed from the conflict, have a right to criticize Israel as we just did on the board? Why or why not? Where do we draw the line of who can and can't criticize Israel?

Criticizing Israel: A Debate Activity

Criticizing Israel

Benjamin Sheridan is a staunch supporter of Israel. A college student in New York, Sheridan has an Israeli flag hanging in his dorm room, sports a wristband that says "Israel is strong" in Hebrew, and is active in his university's Hillel. Or, rather, he was active in Hillel, the campus Jewish-student group, until he was asked to resign from Hillel leadership after he brought a Palestinian activist to speak on campus.

In 2012, Sheridan organized a screening of the documentary *5 Broken Cameras*, an Academy Award–nominated film about Palestinian activism. In conjunction with the showing, Sheridan arranged a talk with Iyad Burnat, the filmmaker's brother and star of the documentary. Although Sheridan openly disagrees with Burnat's anti-Israel views, he saw the event as an opportunity to hear a different perspective on the issue.

> Some Israel supporters feel that open dialogue with Israel's critics can increase understanding and awareness of other viewpoints.

However, the students at Binghamton University's Hillel felt that a speaker who rejects Israel's right to exist shouldn't be given a forum to spread his ideology. Since the group's official policy prohibits partnering with any speaker who promotes the Boycott, Divestment, and Sanctions Movement against Israel (also called BDS, a campaign found on many college campuses that advocates putting economic and political pressure on Israel), Sheridan was asked to step down from Hillel's executive board for inviting the Palestinian activist to campus.

Open Dialogue

The disagreement between Sheridan and Hillel is typical of the current debate over whether and how to criticize the State of Israel and its policies. Like Sheridan, some Israel supporters feel that open dialogue with Israel's critics can increase understanding and awareness of other viewpoints, leading to a broader grasp of the complicated issues and, ultimately, a more effective peace process.

"I still fundamentally disagree with Iyad Burnat," said Sheridan in a written statement to Binghamton's student newspaper, "but the monopoly on political discourse that Hillel at Binghamton conveys is infinitely more dangerous than anything Iyad said in his presentation."

Fairness and Legitimacy

Other Israel supporters believe that delegitimization and demonization of Israel are not reasonable perspectives to be included in the discussion of Israel's policies. They argue that any conversation

Source: Today's Hot Topics · © Behrman House
Image courtesy of Shutterstock, Alexander Ryabintsev

about the Israeli-Palestinian conflict must be built on the premise that Israel has the right to exist, and to exist as a Jewish state.

"Criticism of Israel is important," wrote Alan Dershowitz, professor of law at Harvard University, "as is criticism of any imperfect democracy." But that criticism, he argued, must be built on a foundation of fairness and recognition o Israel's legitimacy, rather than bigotry. "There is a difference," continued Dershowitz, "between mere criticism of Israel and singling it out for unique sanctions such as divestiture or boycott."

Instead of promoting dialogue, argues Dershowitz, giving anti-Israel speakers like Burnat the podium enables them to promote their damaging messages about Israel. As Maya Yair, also a stude at Binghamton University, put it, "Boycotting, dives and sanctions of a country are not dialogue."

What Do You Think?

Who do you think should be included in the ongoing exchange of ideas about Israel's policies?

Chapter 8 It's Creative and Innovative

Words to Know:

capitalism: an economic system in which businesses are owned by private individuals or corporations rather than by the government

Introduction

Enduring Understanding:

Israel encourages entrepreneurship and out-of-the-box thinking, developing technology and inventions used around the world.

Chapter Overview:

This chapter explores some of the many inventions and technologies that have come out of Israel, as well as Israeli innovations in art, entertainment, and fashion. It examines how Israel's government helped foster this culture of innovation and the role community networks play in allowing the culture to thrive. Students will learn how Israeli's acceptance of failure encourages resiliency. Students will also understand that despite the thriving economy, there is still inequity and poverty in Israel.

Chapter 8 Lesson 1

Innovation and Economic Success

Essential Question: How has the Israeli government's investment in creating a capitalist system led to Israeli innovation and economic success?

Learning Objectives: Students will be able to:

- Explain steps the Israeli government has taken to foster a culture of innovation and creativity.
- Describe the impact this has had on the Israeli economy.
- Identify examples of Israeli inventions that are used around the world.

Materials:

- timer
- random objects found in the classroom
- "Toy" video at bhlink.me/israel8 (optional)
- printouts of photos of Israeli products from Etsy.com (students should print these out in advance of class; directions are on page 85 of the student book)

Activities

What Do You See? (5 minutes)

Have students look at the pictures at the bottom of page 80 of *Israel...It's Complicated* and discuss the following questions with a friend:

1. Which of these items do you think is the most exciting product?
2. Which one do you think was the most challenging to invent? Why?

Building Activity: Unintended Consequences

Say to the class:

Sometimes, one innovation has consequences that no one could have anticipated or imagined. For example, a 2008 study wanted to know why Israeli children were much less likely than Jewish children in England to have peanut allergies. Turns out that most Israeli children eat Bamba, an Israeli peanut-puff snack, and researchers credit this with a lower peanut allergy rate. This finding was part of reason for a change in allergy protocols in many countries, including the US and Canada: parents are now encouraged to expose their children to potential allergens earlier to reduce the risk of developing serious allergies. That's quite an accomplishment for a snack!

To read more about the connection between Bamba and peanut allergy research, go to bhlink.me/israel8.

Ask students the following questions:

- How do you think that Osem, the maker of Bamba, felt when it learned that its snack was helping to save kids from peanut allergies? *(Happy that it was helping to keep kids safe; curious about the impact this might have on sales or on the company.)*
- Do you think inventors have a moral or ethical obligation to consider possible implications of their product? If so, how might they initiate that process? *(Some kids might feel that it isn't reasonable to expect companies to predict possible outcomes. Others might say companies should do all they can to ensure no or minimal harm will come from their product. Companies might develop research teams to explore possible outcomes.)*
- Can you think of other examples of innovations with unintended consequences? *(Pesticides that cause disease, social media having political implications, a medication being researched for one disease having positive outcomes for a different illness, etc.)*

Improvise and Innovate (15 minutes)

Divide students into small groups. Then, have them read the text on page 81 of their books and complete the activity there. Before class, ensure there are enough random objects in the room for each group to have five objects to complete step 2.

Ask for one or two volunteers to read steps 1 and 2:

Step 1: Set a timer for five minutes. Each group should try to think of ideas for new inventions of any kind. Make a list of your group's ideas.

Step 2: Collect five random objects from around the room, like a backpack, cardboard box, or a plastic fork. Put them in the middle of your group. Reset the timer for five minutes, and try to come up with a fresh list of ideas—new uses for these five objects. For example, you can use the fork to comb your hair, or you can use the box as a pet carrier to hold a puppy. Write these ideas down on a second list.

After the groups have made their lists, have them discuss the following three questions together:

1. Why is coming up with new ideas difficult? What makes it easier? *(It was hard to come up with something in the beginning, but once we started brainstorming, it was easier to develop new ideas based on those of my classmates.)*

2 Did having the objects in front of you make it easier to innovate? *(Some students might feel that this limited their creativity, since inventions were based on specific objects. Others might have felt that seeing these objects gave them new ideas that they might not otherwise have imagined.)*

3 In what ways do you think having support from the government or investors helps companies innovate? *(Having the resources to hire the right people and purchase needed supplies can make all the difference in moving innovations forward. Additionally, by making it easier to complete necessary legal forms and paperwork, companies can focus on developing and refining their products.)*

Building Activity: The Cutting Edge

Say to students:

> One of the most famous places in Rehovot is the Weizmann Institute of Science, named after Chaim Weizmann, a biochemist, Zionist leader, and the first president of the State of Israel. At the Weizmann Institute, researchers and graduate students conduct advanced studies in mathematics, the sciences, computers, and more. What do you think it might be like to study there? Why might Israel be a great place to study these subjects? *(It would be amazing to study at an institute that has so many leading scholars and researchers working in these fields. There is a lot of high tech in Israel. I would enjoy living in Israel. It would be a challenge to study in Hebrew and to be so far from home.)*

Teacher Tip: If students are interested in learning more about the Weizmann Institute, direct them to the Weizmann Institute web page at bhlink.me/israel8.

Israeli Innovations (10 minutes)

In small groups, ask students to read about the Israeli innovations found on pages 82 to 84 of their books. Then, ask them to create a thirty-second television commercial for one of those products, highlighting that it was developed by Israelis. Share some questions to help students generate ideas for their commercials:

- How might this product help make a difference in the lives of everyday people?
- Why might companies and/or governments want to adopt the use of this product?
- What about life in Israel might have led to this product being developed there?

Students can record their commercials on tablets or smartphones, or perform them in front of the class.

Building Activity: The Music of Israel

Say to students:

Let's watch the video of the song "Toy" (bhlink.me/israel8), by Netta Barzilai, an Israeli singer who won the 2018 Eurovision contest with it. With a partner discuss:

- When you think of Israeli music, is this what comes to mind? Why or why not? *(Students might say that Israeli music encompasses a wide range of musical styles. Others might say that they usually think of more traditional Hebrew songs [like "Yerushalayim shel Zahav"] and were surprised by this type of song.)*
- How do you think Israeli music has been influenced by musicians around the world? *(Musicians get their inspiration from many places. As music evolves in one place, it often influences music everywhere.)*

Creative Crafting: Shopping on Etsy (15 minutes)

Teacher Tip: In advance of class, students should have printed out photos of appealing Israeli products from Etsy.com.

Tell students to turn to page 85 in their books. With their Etsy photos in front of them, working with partners or in small groups, ask them to discuss these questions:

- Why did you pick the product you did? *(Students might pick an object because they like the style, because it reminds them of something they've seen before, because they like wearing Israeli jewelry, or simply because they like the shape or colors.)*
- What about the product is unique and innovative? Did its uniqueness contribute to why you found it appealing? *(Answers will vary based on products chosen, but many students might highlight what makes their item different and why that spoke to them.)*
- Does anything feel Israeli about the product you picked? What makes something "feel Israeli"? *(Students might have an easy time identifying something as Israeli if it has Hebrew on it, depicts a place in Israel like Jerusalem, or is used for Jewish ritual [Shabbat candles or a menorah]. It might be harder to identify something more mundane, like salt and pepper shakers, as Israeli.)*
- Tape or sketch a picture of your product in the space on page 85, and write a short description of it, explaining its appeal to customers. *(Answers will vary based on products chosen.)*

If there's time, pose two more questions to the class:

- Are there any changes you could suggest that would make this product more functional or more attractive to consumers? Write or sketch your ideas around the photo you've taped to or sketched in your book.
- Many consumers are not aware of how many of the products they use every day have roots in Israel. Do you think knowing this information might change their perspective on Israel? If so, how? Why might this matter? *(Since the only things many people hear about Israel involve examples of conflict, highlighting the contributions that Israelis are making to the global economy might change people's views for the better.)*

Chapter 8 Lesson 2

A Culture of Success

Essential Question: How has Israel fostered a culture of innovation, and how can it help those who have been left behind or have chosen not to take part in Israel's economic opportunities?

Learning Objectives: Students will be able to:

- Describe how a culture of learning, a close-knit community, and the contributions of immigrants have helped the Israeli economy to flourish.
- Explain how the courage to fail helps lead to economic success in Israel.
- Articulate that despite the thriving economy, some Israelis still live in poverty.

Materials:

- Markers and/or crayons
- Wooden building blocks (or other stackable items, such as paper cups)
- Timer

Activities

Planting Seeds for Success in Israel (20 minutes)

Teacher Tip: Students will work in small groups for this activity. In advance, make copies of the "Seeds for Success" sheet (found on the following page), one for each group.

Invite volunteers to read aloud "Why Israel?" on page 86 of their books. When they are done, say:

> Take a quick look back at the innovative Israeli products on pages 82 to 84. Imagine that you wanted to continue working on one of these products or invent a new product in the same category. How could a culture of learning, a community network, and immigrants help you achieve this goal?

Divide the class into small groups, and hand each group a "Seeds for Success" sheet (found on page 152). Say:

> As a group, choose one of the Israeli Invention/Innovation items from the list in which you'd like to create a new product or improve an existing product. Circle that subject, and write the product you've agreed upon at the top of the sheet.

After students have written their product idea at the top of the sheet, say:

> Next, circle two or three values that we've studied this year that inspired your creation or that your creation can help achieve.

Then:

> Imagine that you all finished your service in the Israeli army. If you could turn to people in your community network for their advice on your product, whom would you ask for help? What do you think they would tell you to do?
>
> People from different backgrounds bring unique perspectives and skills. How could including immigrants to Israel from the countries on the list or elsewhere help your group?

When students are done, invite the groups to share their inventions/innovations with the rest of the class.

Teacher Tip: This activity could be done as a card game. In advance, write the items of each list on index cards of a different color. Rather than choosing their own category, each group would pick one card from the invention/innovation deck and a predetermined number of cards from the other decks.

Building Activity: *Karish* (Shark) Tank

Ask students to imagine they are business people on a panel deciding whether to fund various entrepreneurs. Give groups a few minutes to plan how to present their products. After each presentation, have members of the panel ask questions, make suggestions for improving the products, and decide whether to fund them.

Failure as a Building Block (10 minutes)

Divide students into small groups. Give each group an equal number of wooden building blocks or other stackable item, such as paper cups. Set the timer for three minutes as students race to build the tallest tower possible.

Afterward, ask students to complete the chart on page 87 and discuss their answers in their groups. Set the timer again for three minutes and have each group build a new tower. The group with the tallest tower at the end of this round wins.

Once the game is complete, discuss the questions beneath the chart in *Israel...It's Complicated* as a group:

1. In what ways did your experience in the first round make your towers more successful the second time? *(We learned what worked and what didn't; we were able to brainstorm a new strategy; we got better at working as a team. If students feel that they were actually less successful the second time, ask them to consider why that might be true.)*
2. Think about a time in your own life when you failed at something. What did you learn from the experience? In what ways did the failure help lead to other successes? *(I learned what worked and what didn't; the failure gave me the confidence to try again; it built up my resilience.)*

Seeds for Success

Israeli Invention/ Innovation	Values Learned	Community Network	Immigrants
communication	creativity	archaeologist	Argentina
conservation	democracy	artist	Canada
medical diagnosis	education	biologist	Ethiopia
medical treatment	freedom	chemist	France
robotics	independence	doctor	Germany
solar	gratitude	engineer	Russia
transportation	home	fund raiser	United Kingdom
water	hope	historian	United States
	peace	marketer	other ______________
	protecting the environment	mathematician	
	religion/belief system	musician	
	respect	rabbi	
	saving a life	sales person	
	self-defense	social worker	
	sharing	soldier	
	understanding one's history	teacher	
	welcoming guests	other ______________	
	Zionism		
	tzedakah		
	other ______________		

Debate It! (10 minutes)

After students have read "Does Israel's Economy Help Everyone?" (page 88 of their books), ask a volunteer to read the directions for the debate at the top of page 89. With a partner, have students take a position and debate the following:

Israel has chosen to invest resources in technology and start-ups. Is that the best choice?

Give pairs a few minutes to debate and write down in their main points:

YES: Israel's choice to invest in technology has helped build a country where many are able to thrive and succeed. (*Without the investment in technology, many more Israelis would be struggling financially, and there would be fewer opportunities for growth. The country has benefited tremendously from its investment in technology. By providing economic growth for so many, additional resources are actually created to help those in need. Many Israelis believe in the mitzvah of tzedakah and will now have the resources to be able to help those in need.)*

NO: The government should be using its resources to help the needy, rather than its corporations. (*Innovators should raise money from private investors, rather than relying on government funding, which should go to help Israelis in need. Alternatively, the government should tax high-earning companies and use the money generated to help the less fortunate.)*

Ask the group:

Which position did you personally think was correct before you debated? Why?

After listening to all the arguments, did your own position change? Why or why not?

Ask for a show of hands, and tally the "Yes" and "No" votes.

Reflections: Talk about It! (5 minutes)

With a friend, discuss the following three questions:

1. Pick three inventions that you learned about in this chapter that were the most interesting to you. What was innovative and unique about them? *(Students will choose products based on their personal interests.)*
2. Compare what you know about Israel's culture of innovation to the culture of your own hometown or school. In what ways are they similar? Different? *(Answer will vary based on where students live. For example, in Seattle there is a strong culture of technology and innovation that has fostered companies like Microsoft and Amazon, similar to the culture in Israel. It's different because there aren't quite the same levels of social connection that help entrepreneurs in Israel.)*
3. What helps you be creative? What can you do to help others be their most innovative and creative? *(What helps me? Listening to music, having quiet time, working with others, reading new books, visiting museums. What helps others? Giving them encouragement and support, helping to pay for supplies and tools, offering to partner with them, even something as simple as offering to bring them food or beverages as they work.)*

Additional Resources

The following activities and information can supplement the lessons or be used on their own to enrich learning about Israel as a place of creativity and innovation.

A Moment of Glee: A Lesson in Inventions Changing Lives

By ISRAEL21c

Introduction

In this lesson, students explore how an Israeli invention that enables wheelchair users to walk (and which appeared on the popular TV show *Glee*) could change someone's life. They learn about the Jewish value to help the disabled and consider how to apply it in real life.

Activity

Part 1: Distribute the "Moment of Glee" article (found on the following pages) and have students read it, either alone or with a partner.

Then, discuss the following questions:

- What will people think about Israel when they watch this TV show and hear that the exoskeleton was invented in Israel?
- Do you think the invention reflects Israeli/Jewish values? How?
- What kind of pressures do you think Artie deals with as a high school kid who is wheelchair-bound?
- How do you think this system would physically and emotionally change the daily life of a person previously confined to a wheelchair?
- What does it mean "to meet the world on the same level"? Why does it matter?

Part 2: With a partner, have students read the following texts and answer the questions that follow:

> **Morning Blessings**
>
> Blessed are You, God our Adonai, Ruler of the world,
> who straightens up those who are bent down.

- What do you think it means to straighten up someone who is bent? Give some concrete examples.
- As people, we are supposed to imitate God. What are some ways in which we can straighten up those who are bent, literally and figuratively?
- How does Goffer's invention of the exoskeleton relate to this blessing?

> **Leviticus 19:14**
>
> You shall not curse the deaf, nor put a stumbling block before
> the blind; you shall be in awe of your God: I am Adonai.

- Why does the Torah command us not to curse the deaf or put a stumbling block before the blind?
- How does this verse tell us to relate to people with disabilities?
- How is the first half of the verse related to the second half of the verse (you shall be in awe of your God: I am God)?
- How did Goffer fulfill this commandment when he made his invention?
- How can we fulfill this commandment better in our own lives?

Part 3: Have students imagine that they are Israeli. They are going to invent something to help the disabled and Israel will become famous for their invention. What would that invention be?

Give each student or pair markers and paper to describe and illustrate the invention. If there is time, students can walk around and look at the other groups' inventions when they have finished their own.

A Moment of Glee

A Moment of Glee

By Israel 21c

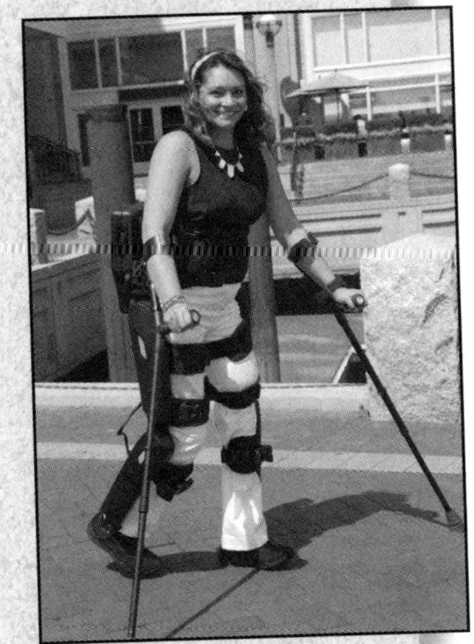

Photo courtesy of ReWalk Robotics

When Artie Abrams, the disabled member of West McKinley High School's Glee club gets up and walks on the program's Christmas special with the aid of a robotic exoskeleton, there isn't a dry eye in the house.

"It was invented by some guy in Israel," says Artie, played by actor Kevin McHale, one of the popular TV show's most endearing characters, a paraplegic teenager who knows how to belt out a great tune.

It's a poignant moment for viewers who have watched Artie deal with the pressures of being wheelchair-bound in an able-bodied and deeply prejudiced society. But for Argo Medical Technologies, the Israeli company that created this unique technology that gives wheelchair users the opportunity to walk, climb stairs and meet the world eye to eye, the show, which aired in the US this week, marks a significant turning point in the company's history.

ISRAEL21c first wrote about Argo Medical in July 2008. It was the first time the company, then a seven-year-old start up, had been featured in the press, and the team behind the quasi-robotic exoskeleton which includes leg braces with motorized joints and motion sensors, a brace support suit and a backpack with a computer and battery, were interested to see what kind of response the device would get.

Standing in line for interviews

Little did they realize what they were in for. The ISRAEL21c story was quickly picked up by popular blogs like MedGadget, Gizmodo, and Engadget, as well as blogs serving the disabled community. Soon after Reuters followed up with a video of the device.

The story exploded on the world's press, and was reported everywhere from Canada's National Post, to Italy's Corriere della Serra. Over 14 TV stations ran their own stories on the technology, from ABC News, to the BBC and CNN. The Israeli company even got coverage in the Teheran Times.

"It all started with ISRAEL21c," says Uri Attir, who was the CEO of Argo Medical in 2008. "This was the first public exposure of Argo. The article gave way to four or five dozen articles and videos. It led the way to everyone standing in line, literally, to interview or film, or both."

Since that first wave of interest, the company has been working hard to develop and test the technology with clinical trials at the Moss Rehabilitation Center in Philadelphia in the US and at the Rehabilitation Hospital at Chaim Sheba Medical Center – Tel Hashomer in Israel.

The 12-employee company has already received CE approval for Europe, and has FDA approval for use in rehabilitation centers. FDA approval for personal use is expected to follow soon.

An unexpected call from Glee

A month ago, according to Oren Tamari, Argo's chief operating officer, the company got an unexpected call from the producers of *Glee*.

A week later the episode was filmed and on Tuesday of this week, American audiences saw Artie walk using the device, called ReWalk. "It's Christmas magic," Tamari tells ISRAEL21c. "They approached us and it all happened very fast."

Aside from enabling users to walk, using crutches for stability and support, the seven-pound device also treats some of the cardiovascular, digestive and circulatory health complications which many wheelchair users suffer.

Designed by a quadriplegic

The exoskeleton has a moving story of its own. It was the brainchild of an Israeli electrical engineer, Dr. Amit Goffer who was left quadriplegic after an accident. He decided to develop a system that allows wheelchair users to walk, climb stairs and meet the world on the same level.

After intensive rehabilitation, Goffer began developing the ReWalk prototype in his home, funding it privately and with a Tnufa – Startup Promotion Program grant. He later entered the Technion Incubator, TechnionSeed for a two-year stint and got financing from VC funds, Vitalife, ProSeed, TechnionSeed, the Technion R&D Foundation, and the Office of the Chief Scientist.

"What we want to do is have the person wake up in the morning, put on clothes, put on the ReWalk, go to work and go throughout the day, wearing it," Goffer, the founder and director of Argo, told ISRAEL21c in 2008.

Now based in Yokneam in Israel's north, the company's target market is the community of wheelchair users in the Western world, of which 300,000 are spinal cord injury sufferers (125,000 in the US and 175,000 in ROW) who are physically able to use crutches as a stabilizing tool.

***Mad About You* star, mad about ReWalk**

Aside from the massive press interest, the ReWalk has also attracted the interest of other Hollywood stars. In April 2009, Paul Reiser, the star of 1990s hit TV show *Mad About You*, saw ISRAEL21c's article and was intrigued enough to follow it up with a visit to the company with his family.

While ReWalk holds out hope for thousands of people, sadly the man who devised the system still cannot benefit from his own invention. Goffer has partial use of his hands, but it is not enough to operate the ReWalk.

In his interview with ISRAEL21c in 2008, Goffer said: "This isn't the first company I've founded. My incentive to develop it was a business opportunity. When I was injured the first thing I was offered was the only thing: a wheelchair. I do believe that in the future, in many cases, the ReWalk – or its competition – might be offered. I don't see any reason for the wheelchair to be the sole solution. There hasn't been a real change [in the technology] for centuries.

"We're taking a safe business approach, starting with paraplegics, and the time for a quadriplegic like me will come," he added.

Back at *Glee*, some attribute the generous present to Artie as a present from Beiste, the high school football coach. Others are calling it a Christmas miracle.

Source: ©Behrman House, 2013

By the Numbers

Poverty Rate in Israel

Poverty is high, particularly among Israeli-Arabs and Haredim

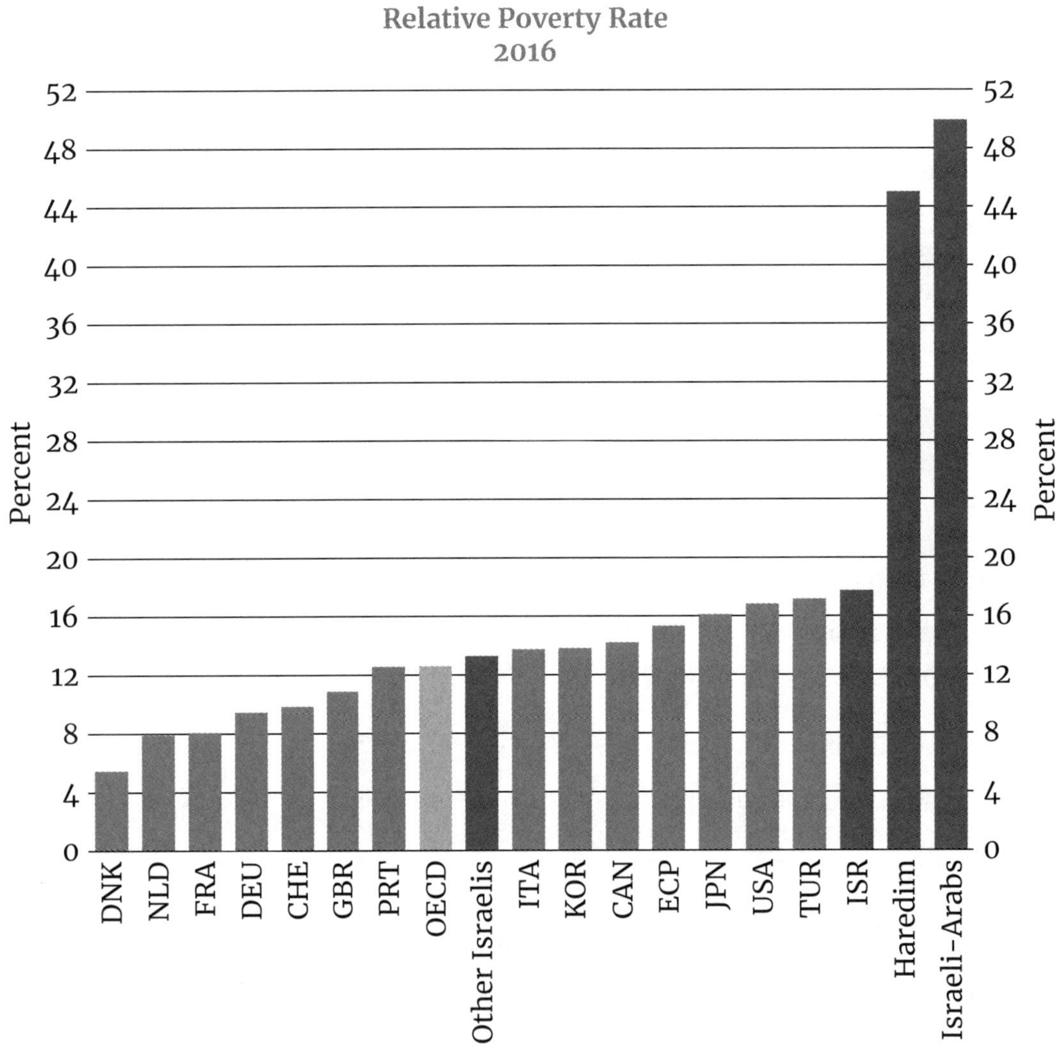

The relative poverty rate measures the share of households whose income is below the threshold of 50% of median disposable income.

Source: OECD (2017), *Income Distribution Database* and National Insurance Institute (2017), *Poverty and Social Gaps Report*, 2016.

Chapter 9 It's a Place to See

Words to Know:

voluntourism: visiting a destination with the intent of spending time there volunteering

Introduction

Enduring Understanding:

People from all over the world visit Israel for the amazing sights, delicious food, and the chance to help others.

Chapter Overview:

This chapter introduces students to Israel as a tourist destination, encouraging them to explore different sites throughout the country. Students will imagine they are tour leaders creating itineraries for a trip to Israel. They will choose places to visit, plan menus, and learn about voluntourism options in Israel.

Chapter 9 Lesson 1
Where in Israel?

Essential Question: From desert hospitality in the footsteps of Abraham and Sarah to whitewater rafting on the Jordan River, what are the sites a visitor to Israel would most enjoy?

Learning Objectives: Students will be able to:

- Explain why people visit Israel.
- Highlight some of the most popular historic destinations in Israel.
- Highlight some of the most popular recreational activities in Israel.

Materials:

- Slips of paper with the name of each site students will explore in their books, placed in a small bag or box. A list of sites can be found below in "Explore Israel."
- Smartphones or tablets for scanning QR codes. (Newer phones will automatically scan QR codes with the camera. If using an older phone or tablet, download the free QR app from the AppStore or Google Play.)
- Map of Israel (one for each student), found on page 170 of this guide.
- Modeling clay (optional)

Activities

Getting Started (5 minutes)

Ask students:

> Have any of you ever been to Israel? If so, what is one thing you remember from your visit? If not, what is one place you'd like to visit in Israel if you had the opportunity to do so?

Students can share their answers with the class.

Explore Israel (35 minutes)

Here is a list of the sites featured on pages 92 through 97 of the student book:

Kotel	Jordan River Rafting and Jeeping
Virtual Reality Second Temple Tour	Dead Sea
Shrine of the Book	Genesis Land
Machane Yehudah	Dig for a Day
Yad Vashem	Sandboarding in the Desert
Tayelet	Masada
Diaspora Museum	Dolphin Reef

Have students, individually or with a partner, to reach into the hat or box you've prepared and pull out a slip of paper with the name of one of these sites on it. Using phones or tablets, have students scan the QR code in the book associated with that site to begin learning about and researching it.

After students have completed their research, including where their site is located, ask them to imagine that they are at a conference of Israeli tour guides. Hand out the maps of Israel, and have students arrange their seats in a circle. Invite each "tour guide" (or pair) to do a short presentation for the rest of the guides about the site he or she has picked. At the beginning of each presentation, students should write the name and location of the site near the accompanying photo and QR code in their books and mark the location of the site on their maps.

Teacher Tip: Remind students to present their information enthusiastically, as though they've actually visited the site.

Teacher Tip: Save students' maps for the Building Activity in lesson 2, "Where Should We Go First?" (optional)

Building Activity: Visit Me

Invite students to create print ads or videos for the tourist site they researched. Display the ads around the room or upload videos to the class website.

Building Activity: Rooftop Tour of Jerusalem

Watch the video "A Rooftop Tour of Jerusalem" together as a group. The video can be found at: bhlink.me/israel9.

Working in small groups, have students choose one of the sites mentioned on the video and research online to answer such questions as: what does it look like (both inside and outside)? What happened there and when? What was the historical context? Which famous people are involved and what was their role?

Using modeling clay, have each group make a small model of their site

Then, guided by the map of Jerusalem, found on page 169 of this guide, assemble the various clay models in the correct place relative to the other sites. If you choose, have students add other landmarks in Jerusalem, too. When the students are done with their work, they will have created a model of the Old City of Jerusalem and the surrounding area that one can look at from above, just as the people in the video looked at Jerusalem from the rooftops.

Each group can present its site and give a brief description of its history.

Display or distribute the following text:

> The Land of Israel is situated in the center of the world,
> and Jerusalem in the center of the Land of Israel.
> —**Midrash Tanhuma, Kedoshim 10**

Then, discuss the following questions:

- *Given what you have learned today about Jerusalem, why do you think the Midrash says that Jerusalem is in the center of the world?*
- *Why do you think Jews pray in the direction of Jerusalem?*
- *How do you connect to Jerusalem, if at all?*

Star Sites (5 minutes)

Invite students to draw a star in their books next to the sites in Israel they'd most like to visit.

Chapter 9 Lesson 2

Follow Me

Essential Questions: If you could plan a trip to Israel, which sites would you visit? What new flavors would you like to taste in Israel?

Learning Objectives: Students will be able to:

- Formulate an itinerary for a trip to Israel.
- Identify ancient, modern, religious, natural, and other sites that would appeal to a variety of tourists to Israel.
- Appreciate that Israeli cuisine is made up of food from around the world

Materials:

- large Post-it Note (optional)
- ingredients for an Israeli dish / Israeli dips and vegetables (optional)

Activities

Getting Started (5 minutes)

Ask students to look through the sites they starred on pages 92 through 97 of their books. What is the top site they'd like to visit in Israel? Invite students to write the name of that site on the board, white board, or a large Post-it Note. Tally the class's favorite sites.

Design a Tour (25 minutes)

As they did in the previous lesson, students will imagine that they are tour guides. Invite a volunteer to read "Design a Tour" at the top of page 91. Have students complete step 1, identifying their customers and the theme for their trip to Israel.

Give students several minutes to review all the sites on pages 92 through 97. For each site, ask them to circle in their books whether they would include it in their itinerary and why or why not.

Next, ask students to complete the itinerary on page 98 of their books, writing the theme at the top of the page, and listing their top five sites that fit that theme. They will also recommend a Jewish site, a historical site, a modern site, a cultural site, and a nature site.

Then, ask students to share their itinerary with a friend and discuss the following questions:

1. Why did you pick the activities that you did for your customers? *(Because they sounded interesting, they looked fun, they feel like an essential part of the Israel experience, because a friend went there and enjoyed it....)*
2. Which of the sites did you put stars next to? What about them was most appealing to you? *(Answers will vary based on student response.)*
3. Which of the sites that your friend picked would you most want to visit? Why? *(Answers will vary based on student response.)*

Building Activity: Where Should We Go First?

Using the maps from lesson 1 on which they've plotted all the tourist sites they learned about, ask students to circle all the sites they've included in their itineraries and figure out the most sensible route, beginning in Jerusalem, for their one-week tour.

Building Activity: Trip Advisor

Say to students:

> Imagine you visited your top site in Israel. Why was it so great? Write a review and give it one to five Jewish stars, depending on how much it lived up to your expectations.

Plan Your Menu (15 minutes)

Say to students:

> Part of any vacation is enjoying the food. If you were visiting Israel, where would you want to eat?

Ask students to imagine that they and their friends are stopping for dinner in Tel Aviv. In small groups, have them use computers or smartphones to visit bhlink.me/israel9 to see different Tel Aviv restaurant menus. Ask them to create their perfect meals by picking one dish from the different menus—an appetizer, a main dish, a side dish, and a dessert—and writing their choices in the spaces on page 99 of their student books.

Then, ask students to discuss the following questions with a partner:

- What countries or cultures do you think influenced the dishes that you chose for your meal? *(Answers will vary based on student response.)*
- Which dish that you chose is the most "Israeli"? Why do you think so? (*(Answers will vary based on student response, but students might feel that all the dishes are part of the diversity of Israel or that their dishes don't actually reflect Israeli cuisine.)*

Building Activity: Cook It!

You might choose to cook an Israeli dish with your class (you can easily find recipes online) or bring in an assortment of Israel dips and vegetables.

Teacher Tip: Check with your education director, principal, or rabbi to ensure that you are meeting the kashrut needs of your community (if applicable), and that financial resources exist to purchase food and supplies. Keep in mind any allergies your students may have.

Chapter 9 Lesson 3
Voluntourism

Essential Question: How can you make a difference in the lives of Israelis on a trip to Israel?

Learning Objectives: Students will be able to:

- Articulate social justice issues that matter to them.
- Define voluntourism.
- Identify voluntourism opportunities in Israel.

Lesson at a Glance: Students will consider what social justice issues are important to them and how they might pursue these interests while engaging in voluntourism in Israel.

Activities

Getting Started (10 minutes)

Ask students:

Have you ever participated in a service / mitzvah project? If so, what kind?

Give students a few minutes to share their answers with the class. Then, write the word *Voluntourism* on the board and ask students to define it. Why do they think this would be a fun/important activity to do when visiting Israel?

Making a Difference (25 minutes)

Have a volunteer read aloud the first paragraph of "Making a Difference" at the top of page 101. Hand out paper and pens/pencils to students; ask them to each make a list of social justice issues that are important to them.

Then, in groups of two or three, ask students to discuss the four questions in their books:

1. Would you like to work with people or animals?
2. Would you prefer to do work that uses your mind (like creating something) or work that uses your body (like clearing a nature trail)?
3. What would you hope to learn from your experience?
4. What skills do you have to offer (for example, good with children, skilled at computers)?

Finally, have students visit bhlink.me/israel9 and look at the links for Leket Israel, Keren Or Jerusalem Center for Blind Children with Multiple Disabilities, Pantry Packers, and other organizations in Israel that accept volunteers. Based on their lists and the voluntourism opportunities they just read about online, ask students to fill in the boxes on page 101 of their books with the name of the project on which they'd like to volunteer on a trip to Israel and the reasons they would choose that project.

End by inviting students to share their choices and their reasons with the class.

Building Activity: Volunteerism at Home

Teacher Tip: This activity requires approval from your education director, principal, or rabbi, as well as parents, before proposing it to the class. If it is not possible to volunteer as a class, students can, instead, exchange ideas about local programs with which they're familiar.

Say to the class:

> *Now that you've discussed which social justice issues are important to you, can we figure out a way to help one of these causes in our own community?*

As a class, choose a project similar to one of the voluntourism projects your students learned about, a food pantry or meal center, for example, or choose another local project in which to get involved as a class.

Building Activity: A Year of Volunteering

Hand out a sheet of paper and a pen/pencil to each student. Tell students to fold the paper in quarters and at the top of each quarter, write a season of the year: Fall, Winter, Spring, Summer. Brainstorming with a partner, have students list as many social justice or service projects they can think of for each season of the year. Remind them that some projects are important all year round. *(A gently-used sports equipment drive for seasonal sports; fall and spring, playing sports with special-needs children; winter, arts and crafts or music with special-needs children; winter, coat drive; spring, planting a vegetable garden to be harvested for a food pantry; year-round, stocking a food pantry)*

Reflections: Talk about It! (10 minutes)

With a partner, have students discuss the following questions, some of which are found at the bottom of page 101 of *Israel...It's Complicated.*

- If you have ever been to Israel, describe the most memorable experience you had there. If you have not been there, whom do you know who has visited? What have they told you about their experiences?
- Whom do you know that might not enjoy a visit to Israel? Why do you think they wouldn't? Knowing all you now know about Israel, how do you think you could persuade that person to think more positively about visiting?
- Whom do you know that you think would get the most out of a visit to Israel? Why do you think so?

(Due to the personal nature of these questions, answers will vary depending on student interests.)

Go around the room and ask students to name the top place they'd like to visit in Israel, the one food they really want to try in Israel, and the voluntourism project in which they'd most like to participate.

Additional Resources

The following activities and information can supplement the lessons or be used on their own to enrich learning about Israel as a tourist destination.

By the Numbers

Annual Tourists to Israel

YEAR	# of Tourist Arrivals
2007	2,063,100
2008	2,568,600
2009	2,321,400
2010	2,803,100
2011	2,820,200
2012	2,885,900
2013	2,961,700
2014	2,926,700
2015	2,799,500
2016	2,900,000
2017	3,613,200
2018	4,120,800

Source: Central Bureau of Statistics, State of Israel

Old City of Jerusalem

Map courtesy of Wikimedia Commons

Major Places in Israel

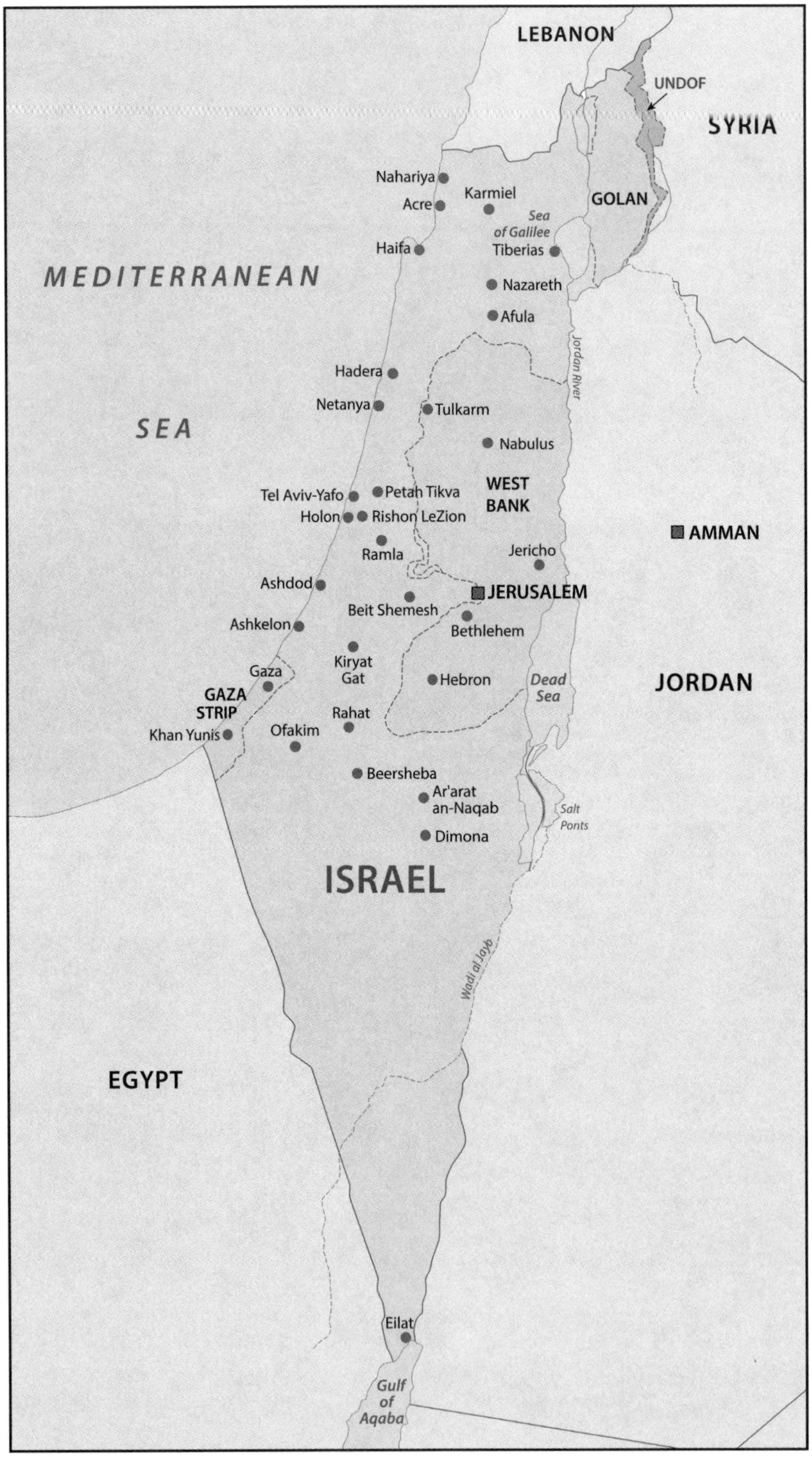

Map courtesy of Shutterstock

NFTY Teen Trip Itinerary

NFTY in Israel

Teen Adventure Trip Itinerary

Wednesday, June 20: B'ruchim Habaim L'Yisrael!—Welcome to Israel!

Tel Yafo—a lookout point over ancient Jaffa, the historic arrival point for thousands of pilgrims to the land of Israel. See firsthand how immigrants from around the world came to Israel and created the Jewish State.

Thursday, June 21: Genesis

Map orientation program. Visit an archaeological dig.

Friday, June 22: Exodus

For the next three days, we will be trekking through the desert just as our ancestors did during the Biblical Period on their exodus from Egypt to the Land of Israel. Visit to Sde Boker, the home of Israel's first Prime Minister, David Ben-Gurion. Sleep under the stars.

Saturday, June 23: Shabbat

Early morning hike, followed by *tefillah* in the desert and then enjoy a relaxing afternoon break at Eilat's fantastic Coral Beach, where we will take snorkels and dive into the cool water of the Red Sea. *Havdallah* and a night program under the stars.

Sunday, June 24: Am Yisrael

Continue hiking and marvel at the breathtaking views, tenacious plants and extraordinary wildlife. Understand how time in the desert served as a tool for shaping and creating *Am Yisrael* (the People of Israel).

Monday, June 25: Jerusalem of Gold

Start the day in Kibbutz Yahel where we will return our desert gear and have lunch. Then drive to Jerusalem. Visit Tayelet: a lookout point over the Old City of Jerusalem.

Tuesday, June 26: Ancient Jerusalem

Shop and explore in Jerusalem's open-air market, Machaneh Yehuda, followed by a picnic lunch. Walking into the Old City of Jerusalem.. Water-hike through an ancient underground aqueduct built by King Hezekiah to defend Jerusalem from the Assyrians in 722 BCE. Visit the Kotel.

Wednesday, June 27: The Fall of Jerusalem

Learn about the tragic Fall of Jerusalem in 70 CE. Visit the Burnt House, see the actual charred remains of the great fire that burned Jerusalem to the ground on *Tisha B'Av*. At the Last Supper Room on Mount Zion we will learn about the birth of Christianity during the chaos of the last days of the Second Temple in Jerusalem. Eat dinner and sleep in a Bedouin tent.

Thursday, June 28: Masada

Sunrise hike to climb Masada.

NFTY Teen Trip Itinerary (continued)

Friday, June 29: Rabbinic Judaism

Tzippori, an ancient city that was the most important city in the Galilee in the first four centuries CE.

Saturday, June 30: Shabbat in Akko

Sunday, July 1: Islam and The Crusades

Visit a beautiful mosque and learn about the similarities and differences between Judaism and Islam.

Sunday, July 1 - Wednesday, July 4: Chavayot

Options include:

Tikkun Olam. Projects may include working with new immigrants, special needs children or the elderly.

Gadna (Army Training). Participate in simulated basic army exercises, while living on an Israeli Army base.

Yam L'Yam (Sea to Sea). A challenging four-day trek from the Sea of Galilee to the Mediterranean Sea. Gain experience climbing, orienteering, and hiking, mountain biking and camping, every night out under the stars..

Thursday, July 5: Kibbutz Pioneers

Learn about the pioneers who rebuilt the land of Israel over the last century. Visit the Kinneret Cemetery to learn about some of these great pioneers. Swim in the Sea of Galilee.

Friday, July 6: Kabbalah Mystics

Hike the Arbel Nature Reserve overlooking the Sea of Galilee. Travel to the beautiful, mystical city of Tzfat, high up in the mountains.

Saturday, July 7: Shabbat

Sunday, July 8: Israeli Peers

Today, our Israeli peers are joining our group. Spend time at the beach, going out on banana boats and enjoying the cool waters of the Sea of Galilee. After dinner cultural program about Israeli music.

Monday, July 9: Borders

Visit the Golan Heights where we will see both the beauty of the landscape and its history of war and struggle. Cool off while rafting on the Chatzbani River.

Tuesday, July 10: Coexistence

Go to the Druze Village of Dalyat HaCarmel. After lunch, we will go to Bat Hefer, an Israeli town adjacent to Israel's security fence.

Wednesday, July 11: Memory

Visit Yad Vashem, Israel's Holocaust memorial.

Thursday, July 12: Tel Aviv – Old New Land

Travel to the Weizmann Institute in Rehovot. No less than 6 Nobel Prize laureates have been associated with this prestigious institute. Swim at one of Tel Aviv's beautiful beaches.

Friday, July 13: HaTikvah – The Hope

Travel back in time to Independence Hall, where the State of Israel declared its statehood in 1948. Visit the *Shuk HaCarmel*, Tel Aviv's open-air fresh food market.

Saturday, July 14: Shabbat

Sunday, July 15: Shalom-Peace?

Visit with an Arab family in Ein Rafa, an Arab village, where we will learn about the historical connections of the Arabs and of Islam to the city of Jerusalem and the land of Israel. Visit Mount Herzl, the national cemetery.

Monday, July 16: Taking Israel Back Home

Prepare to travel home.

Itinerary courtesy of Union for Reform Judaism, NFTY

Hiking Across All of Israel

Step Out on the Israel Trail

By Yehezkel Laing, ISRAEL21c

Hikers on the Israel Trail.
Photo by Yoav Dothan, Wikimedia Commons

Just how small is the State of Israel? Small enough for thousands of people every year to cross the entire length of the country by foot power alone. They do it via a special hiking path called the Israel National Trail (INT) or Israel Trail for short ("Shvil Yisrael" in Hebrew) that winds its way over almost 1,000 kilometers (580 miles) of terrain.

Starting in Metulla, on the northern border next to Lebanon, the trail finishes in Eilat, at Israel's southern tip on the Red Sea. While many countries have hiking trails crossing large portions of their land, Israel is believed to be the only country in the world to offer a trail crossing its entire length without interruption.

Incredible geographical diversity

It's been said that the Holy Land comprises a wider variety of landscapes in less space than anywhere in the world, and nothing proves that better than the Israel Trail. The INT comprises all the wonders that Israel has to offer. Crammed into its length are snow-capped mountains, desert craters, forested hills, Lake Kinneret, the Mediterranean Sea coastline with its sandy beaches and more.

The trail also provides a cornucopia for history buffs, allowing hikers to walk in the footsteps of the Israelite tribes, ancient kings and religious leaders, with ample archeological discoveries to see along the way. "The biggest draw is the scenery," says Gal Hart, an Israel Trail administrator. "In other counties the landscape may change every few weeks of hiking. In Israel the landscape changes radically every day or two, providing a feast for the senses."

For many, the Israel Trail is more than just a nature hike. It's a way to escape the rat race, slow time down and connect with Israel – its land and people — on a primal level in a single embrace. Walking at a regular pace, the average hiker can finish the entire route in one to two months. Strong hikers have been known to finish in only three weeks.

The trail has also been subdivided to allow for shorter journeys. Hundreds of hiking groups walk these smaller portions of the trail every month, until they complete the entire length over two years.

The Society for the Protection of Nature in Israel recommends hiking when temperatures are most moderate, in the fall and spring. While essentially a nature route, the path frequently passes by towns, enabling easy resupply of provisions.

Appalachian inspiration

Though it long ago achieved legendary status, the trail is actually less than 20 years old. Like many great projects, it began with a vision. While hiking the American Appalachian Trail in 1980, Israeli journalist Avraham Tamir had an inspiration: Why not build a similar trail crossing the entire land of Israel?

When he got back home, he went straight to SPNI director Ori Devir, who fell in love with the concept. Though the trail was mostly made by joining together existing hiking routes, it still took more than 15 years to complete. In 1995 it was finally inaugurated.

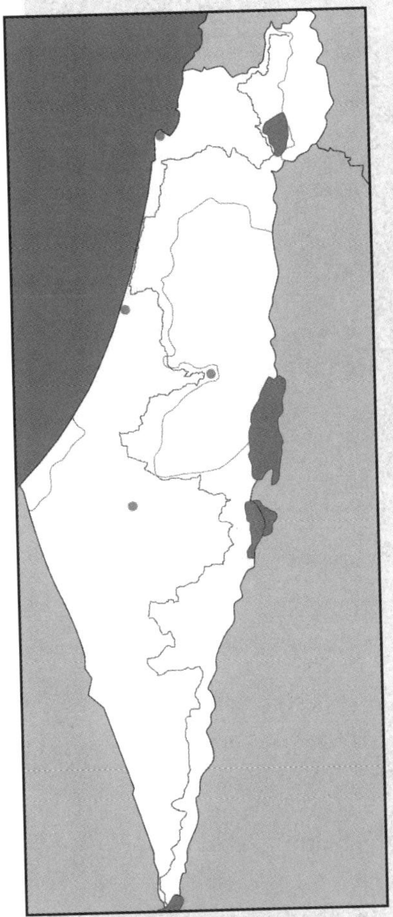

The Israel Trail runs the entire length of Israel, from the northern border with Lebanon to the southern tip in Eilat.
Map courtesy of Wikimedia Commons.

"Many embark on the trail to mark the end of a special event or the beginning of a new one," says Hart.

It's common, for instance, for Israeli soldiers who have finished their mandatory three-year service to celebrate their discharge by hiking the trail. Newlyweds walk it for their honeymoons, married couples on their anniversaries and younger hikers to mark their bar or bat mitzvah.

Baruch Kronbain, 26, from Moshav Margaliot near Kiryat Shmonah in the north, is a social work student at Tel-Hai College. He did the trail four years ago after completing his military service. "I hiked with two army buddies from Metulla to Mitzpe Ramon. We hiked during the winter, which is less common due to the wet weather. But the most memorable part for me was actually when we hiked and slept outside during a downpour."

The trail is also popular with foreign tourists. Last year, former action movie star Chuck Norris, a committed Christian Zionist, hiked the entire length with his wife Tigger, who kept an extensive online blog of their journey.

Path to companionship

Camaraderie between hikers is high. Veterans of the trail are known as "shvilistim" or "people of the path." Internet forums let old-timers and newcomers share tips, ideas and experiences.

You can hike the trail north to south or south to north. "Due to the two-way travel, it is common for travelers to meet up with hikers going in the opposite direction overnight over a campfire. This leads to many unique one-night experiences," says Hart.

Other regions, especially the South, are ideal for solitude. For Hart, the most beautiful section was in the Negev between Mitzpe Ramon and the Arava Desert. "There you can walk for over four days through some of the most spectacular scenery and not meet a single soul."

Angels on the trail

A few years ago, SPNI initiated the Trail Angels Program. This group of good Samaritans (most of them veterans of the INT themselves and living in proximity to its path) open their homes to the hikers, providing them with much-appreciated amenities.

Kronbain himself has been an angel for about a year. During that time he has hosted over 50 hikers, all of whom have left their imprint in a guest book he lays out.

"Angels provide hikers with lodging, hot meals, showers, Wi-Fi connectivity and use of the washing machine, all free of charge," he says. Evenings are spent discussing the trail, or singing songs often around a campfire with a guitar. Often the angels aren't even home when the travelers come by, and just leave their doors open with a note saying, "There's food in the fridge. Take whatever you need!"

Birding in Israel

Birds of a Feather Flock to Israel

By Abigail Klein Leichman for ISRAEL21c

At least 500 million birds of 200 different species fly across Israel each spring and autumn en route to and from Africa, Europe and Asia. And more than 70 native Israeli species, such as the hoopoe (its national bird since 2008), cuckoo, Egyptian vulture, short-toed eagle, hobby and lesser kestrel, often head to warmer Africa in winter.

Blue rock thrush at Gamla Nature Reserve.
Photo by Artemy Voikhansky, Wikimedia Commons

Hordes of birdwatchers from across the globe flock to strategic locations along the migratory route twice every year to take in this extraordinary sight. And all year long, naturalists work hard to preserve flyways, gather data on the visiting birds and teach adults and kids how to make these feathered friends feel welcome.

Award winning Israeli ornithologist Yossi Leshem heads the International Center for the Study of Bird Migration in central Latrun. ICSBM's many projects range from studying the birds and their habits to protecting them during their long trip. It has a radar warning system for military and commercial pilots aimed at preventing bird strikes, a common danger during takeoff and landing. When planes hit birds at high speeds, these accidents are not only fatal to the birds but also dangerous for pilots and sensitive equipment.

Migrating birds know no boundaries

Leshem worked with Jordan, Greece and Turkey to expand this successful scheme throughout the region, and collaborates with ornithologists in European, Mideast and African countries to study the behavior of migrating birds as a predictor for climate change.

Leshem's slogan, "Migrating birds know no boundaries," was the title of a six-year USAID-Middle East Regional Cooperation Foundation-funded program that established ringing stations and trained Israelis, Palestinians and Jordanians to staff them.

Ringers, also known as banders, capture visiting birds long enough to place an aluminum band around one leg. The band is engraved with contact and ID information so as to monitor them from year to year and place to place.

In another project of the program, schoolchildren in Israel, the Palestinian Authority and Jordan tracked the movement of migrating German white storks fitted with satellite transmitters.

These initiatives have continued and expanded. Israel now has a national network of 10 bird-watching stations run in cooperation with the Israel Ornithology Center, and Leshem is working with Palestinian and Jordanian authorities to attract additional eco-tourists and birdwatchers to the Middle East.

Strategic stopover in Eilat

Once upon a time, the natural salt marsh at the southern tip of Israel was a major "gas station" for birds heading up from Africa in the spring, according to Rea Shaish of the International Birding and Research Center in Eilat.

"After crossing the deserts south of us, they have to refuel," explains Shaish. "They stop every few days to regain their fat sources to support them energetically and stay hydrated."

Overdevelopment caused the marshes to disappear by the 1960s, leaving the migrating birds high and dry. After a couple of decades, the Keren Kayemeth LeYisrael-Jewish National Fund transformed a rubbish heap in the same area into a green sanctuary with freshwater and saline lagoons. And the birds returned.

"We have made it as close as possible to the old salt marsh. Here they have an area in which to rest and refuel without disturbance," Shaish tells ISRAEL21c.

IBRC monitors the effects of environmental changes on banded birds by tracking their movements and migration every year. "We also have an educational project with schools here in Eilat and guided tours for tourists every week, where we explain about ringing, which is our main research tool," says Shaish, who is a ringer, tracker and guide at the facility.

The IBRCE offers a two-week session for volunteers during the autumn and spring migration. They learn how to handle different species as they extract them from traps and nets for ringing, such as swallows, prinias, little stints and shrikes.

At the peak of spring, hundreds of species from Asia and Europe stop by, including large raptors such as steppe eagles, sparrow hawks and white storks. "The dominant species are blackcap warblers, barn swallows and European bee-eaters, one of most colorful birds in Israel," says Shaish.

The center is home to a year-round population of several hundred pink flamingos, adding color to Eilat's 200-plus indigenous species such as sun birds, shrikes and hoop larks.

Some birds winter in Israel

"Our winter is very light and warm, so a lot of migrating birds stay here for the winter," says David Glasner of the International Birdwatching Center of the Jordan Valley at Kfar Ruppin.

Grey herons, black kites, robins, common cranes and ducks are among 94 species of cold-weather visitors providing a dependable population for birdwatchers to enjoy.

"Even the numbers of some resident species in Israel grow during the winter because others come from northern countries like Turkey or Greece," adds Glasner. "We have 350 species on our local checklist, at least 120 of which are wintering birds."

The center has developed and shared strategies to protect the hungry travelers from getting entangled in the nets topping the many commercial fish ponds in the area and from ingesting pesticides as they peck in its vast agricultural fields.

In partnership with Israel's Nature Reserve Authority, IBCJV offers fish farms alternative wide-stringed nets less likely to snare birds. When necessary, its staff rescues, rings and sets free fish-

Birding in Israel (continued)

eating pelicans, cormorants and herons that do get stuck. Any wounded birds are sent for treatment at a hospital in the Ramat Gan Safari.

To keep farmers and birds happy, the best solution has been setting up barn owl and kestrel nesting boxes as part of a national effort to introduce this natural rodent-control method. Reducing pesticide use benefits everyone from the migratory birds to the end consumer.

In another longstanding cooperative venture, the IBCJV partners with Israel Electric to keep larger migrating birds such as pelicans, herons and white storks from getting electrocuted on power lines.

"Our part in this is to find the places where the birds are getting electrocuted and inform the electric company," Glasner tells ISRAEL21c. "They come and install insulation around the high-voltage wires so when the birds sit on the poles and touch the wires with their wings, they do not get electrocuted and do not damage the system."

The center offers real-time bird-watching information for visitors and correspondents, and maintains a rural lodge in walking distance of the bird-watching hot spots on its grounds.

Bird-lovers flock to Israel

"To see the birds of Europe you come to Israel, because they all migrate here," says Jerusalem Bird Observatory manager Alen Kacal. "Israel is one of the best places in the world to view bird migration, along with Panama, Morocco and Gibraltar."

The JBO, Israel's first urban wildlife center, sits between the Knesset and the Supreme Court. Its sheltering trees and shrubs attract the kinds of insects that birds like to eat, and there is a pond for bathing and drinking. Thousands of birds stop here to fill their bellies and rest before continuing their long trek, and some—including many European robins and chaffinches—choose to stay permanently.

The center's ringing operation bands more than 10,000 birds a year and records each one's weight, gender and species. This provides a wealth of information about the feathered visitors.

"If a bird we ringed ends up in Estonia or Kenya, they contact us and tell us where the bird is, and we do the same," she tells ISRAEL21c. "We've been able to make detailed maps of where the birds go, how long it takes them to get there, what their route is and where the most important 'gas stations' are along the way. These are the places we need to preserve."

Human visitors of all ages flock to JBO daily for informal bird-watching as well as lectures, demonstrations and creative art programs.

"We want people to be aware of what's in their backyards, and we want them to make a personal connection with the nature around them," says Kacal. "We also try to make a global connection: The little bird they see here has come from Sweden on a huge journey and if we don't take care of our environment it cannot eat or drink and it will die. So we have a global responsibility."

Where to see migrating birds

The Kibbutz Lotan Ecotourism and Birdwatching Center in the Arava Valley is among several prime bird-watching spots during the spring and fall migrations. Other southern hot spots include the Negev desert, Dead Sea and Eilat. In northern Israel, popular bird-watching areas are the Agamon Hula Ornithology and Nature Park, Kibbutz Ma'agan Michael near the southern Carmel Mountains, and the Beit She'an and Jezreel

Conclusion

What Does Israel Mean to Me?

Introduction

Enduring Understanding:

We each have a personal relationship to Israel, which we can continue to develop by asking questions about, learning more about, and visiting Israel.

Chapter Overview:

Students will create a word association to understand how their learning experiences have impacted their ideas about Israel. Students will be able to express some of the ways in which life in Israel can be complicated and will dream about Israel's future.

Conclusion Lesson 1

Israel and Me: Today and Tomorrow

Essential Question: What does Israel mean to me, and what are my hopes for Israel's future?

Learning Objectives: Students will be able to:

- Identify the words they now associate with Israel, after having studied *Israel: It's Complicated.*
- Explain some of the ways in which life in Israel can be complicated.
- Articulate a dream for Israel's future.

Materials:

- poster board or large paper
- markers
- tape for hanging posters on the wall
- sticky notes

Activities

Design an Israeli Star (5 minutes)

Have a volunteer read step 1 of the directions at the top of page 103 of Israel...It's Complicated. Give students a few minutes to fill in the words they now associate with Israel. Remind them that they should write the words they most strongly associate with Israel larger and the other words smaller.

Then, ask students to compare the words they've written in this star with the words they wrote in the star on page 5 of their books. Which words are new, which words are missing, and which words have changed size?

Ask:

> How do you feel differently about Israel now than you did when we started learning about Israel? ?

What I Know about Israel (30 minutes)

Say to students:

List three complicated questions we studied that helped you understand Israel more deeply. Feel free to look back at previous chapters as a reminder.

(Possible questions:

- *What land is included within Israel's borders?*
- *Who qualifies as Jewish under the Law of Return?*
- *In what ways is Israeli society both diverse and divided?*
- *Israel is a sacred place to many religions. In what way is it challenging to share sacred spaces?*
- *How does Israel struggle to balance Jewish and democratic values and ideals?*
- *What happens when cultural values clash with religious values?*
- *Yom Ha'atzmaut, Israel Independence Day, is a day of celebration for Jews around the world but considered the Nakba (catastrophe) by Palestinians. How can Jews celebrate Yom Ha'atzma'ut and at the same time acknowledge the feelings of the Palestinians?*
- *Why have attempts to make peace between Israel and neighboring countries met with more failures than successes?*
- *Do the West Bank settlements promote security for Israel?*
- *Why, despite Israel's contributions to the world, does it continue to be viewed negatively by so many countries?*
- *Is it okay for Jews to criticize Israel?*
- *Israel has a booming tech economy, yet many Israelis still live in poverty. What role, if any, should the Israeli government play in addressing economic inequality?)*

Then say:

With a partner, review each other's questions. Choose one question from each of your lists, and imagine you had to explain those issues to a person with limited knowledge of Israel. What would you tell him or her? What questions might that person ask? What are your own opinions on the issue? Role-play how the conversation might go. *(Answers will vary based on student responses.)*

If time permits, invite students to share their answers or role plays with the class.

Teacher Tip: You may wish to assign specific questions to students or pairs to ensure that all questions and answers are reviewed by the class.

Building Activity: A New Gallery of Questions

Distribute poster board or large sheets of paper, markers, tape, and sticky notes. In small groups, have students make a list of questions they still have about Israel. Then, ask each group to choose the three questions they find most interesting, copy them onto a poster board or sheet of large paper, and hang them on the wall.

Invite students to go around the room reading each group's questions. Ask them to write their responses to the questions on sticky notes and stick them to the poster.

Responses may include: *New questions that were inspired by the questions on the wall. Possible answers to the questions. Suggestions for how students can learn more about the issues. One-word responses that describe how the questions make students feel (happy; angry; worried; proud)*

Once everyone has posted their notes, have students walk around the room and read all the notes. Then, come back and discuss as a group.

- Which questions surprised students?
- Which questions were similar to their own?
- Were there any questions that they'd like to add to their own lists?
- Were there any questions they'd like to answer?

(Answers will vary based on student response.)

Building Activity: Future Perfect

Say to students:

> Imagine you are speaking to the kids who will use this book next year. What do you think future students will most enjoy learning? What message would you want to give future classes about your experiences studying Israel?

Imagine: A Dream for Israel's Future (10 minutes)

Say to students:

> Imagine it is the year 2050. You are in Israel and want to send a message home that describes what the country and people are like.
>
> What do you think will be the same as it is today? Different? What do you think will be more complicated? Less complicated?
>
> Write an email message on page 102 of your books.
>
> *(Students might write that they hope Israel will have signed peace treaties with more of its neighbors or that service in the IDF is no longer mandatory because of those peace treaties. They might wish for more diversity in Israel, that the Israeli economy has continued to expand, that all forms of Jewish worship are welcomed in Israel. They may think additional complications have arisen due to technological advances, that an increase in population will make it more difficult to find a place to live in Israel and result in increased traffic issues, or that it might be harder to communicate because so many different languages will be spoken in Israel due to increased immigration, etc.)*

Encourage students to share their emails with the class.